Kosovo

This book edition is published by
Zhingoora Books.

The Cover is Designed by Pallav Sethiya.

Kosovo (Europe)

Introduction ::Kosovo

Background:

Ethnic Serbs migrated to the territories of modern Kosovo in the 7th century but did not fully incorporate them into the Serbian realm until the early 13th century. During the medieval period, Kosovo became the center of a Serbian Empire and saw the construction of many important Serb religious sites, including many architecturally significant Serbian Orthodox monasteries. The defeat of Serbian forces at the Battle of Kosovo in 1389 led to five centuries of Ottoman rule during which large numbers of Turks and Albanians moved to Kosovo. By the end of the 19th century, Albanians replaced the Serbs as the dominant ethnic group in Kosovo. Serbia reacquired control over Kosovo from the Ottoman Empire during the First Balkan War of 1912. Kosovo became an autonomous province of Serbia with status almost equivalent to that of a republic under the 1974 Constitution of the Socialist Federal Republic of Yugoslavia. Despite legislative concessions, Albanian nationalism increased in the 1980s, which led to riots and calls for Kosovo's independence. At the same time, Serb nationalist leaders, such as Slobodan MILOSEVIC, exploited Kosovo Serb claims of maltreatment to secure votes from supporters, many of whom viewed Kosovo as their cultural heartland. Under MILOSEVIC's leadership, Serbia instituted a new constitution in 1989 that revoked Kosovo's status as an autonomous province of Serbia. Kosovo Albanian leaders responded in 1991 by organizing a referendum that declared Kosovo independent. Under MILOSEVIC, Serbia carried out repressive measures against the Albanians in the early 1990s as the unofficial Kosovo government, led by Ibrahim RUGOVA, used passive resistance in an attempt to try to gain international assistance and recognition of an independent Kosovo.

Albanians dissatisfied with RUGOVA's passive strategy in the 1990s created the Kosovo Liberation Army and launched an insurgency. Starting in 1998, Serbian military, police, and paramilitary forces conducted a counterinsurgency campaign that resulted in massacres and massive expulsions of ethnic Albanians. Approximately 800,000 Albanians were forced from their homes in Kosovo during this time. International attempts to mediate the conflict failed, and MILOSEVIC's rejection of a proposed settlement led to a three-month NATO military campaign against Serbia beginning in March 1999 that forced Serbia to agree to withdraw its military and police forces from Kosovo. UN Security Council Resolution 1244 (1999) placed Kosovo under a transitional administration, the UN Interim Administration Mission in Kosovo (UNMIK), pending a determination of Kosovo's future status. A UN-led process began in late 2005 to determine Kosovo's final status. The negotiations ran in stages between 2006 and 2007, but ended without agreement between Belgrade and Pristina. On 17 February 2008, the Kosovo Assembly declared Kosovo independent. Since then, over sixty countries have recognized Kosovo, and it has joined the International Monetary Fund and World Bank. Serbia continues to reject Kosovo's independence and it subsequently sought an advisory opinion from the International Court of Justice (ICJ) on the legality under international law of Kosovo's independence declaration. In July 2010 the ICJ ruled that Kosovo's declaration of independence did not violate international law.

Geography ::Kosovo

Location: Southeast Europe, between Serbia and Macedonia

Geographic coordinates: 42 35 N, 21 00 E

Map references: Europe

Area:

Total: 10,887 sq km

Country comparison to the world: 168

Land: 10,887 sq km

Water: 0 sq km

Area - comparative: slightly larger than Delaware

Land boundaries:

Total: 702 km

Border countries: Albania 112 km, Macedonia 159 km, Montenegro 79 km, Serbia 352 km

Coastline: 0 km (landlocked)

Maritime claims: none (landlocked)

Climate: influenced by continental air masses resulting in relatively cold winters with heavy snowfall and hot, dry summers and autumns; Mediterranean and alpine influences create regional variation; maximum rainfall between October and December

Terrain: flat fluvial basin with an elevation of 400-700 m above sea level surrounded by several high mountain ranges with elevations of 2,000 to 2,500 m

Elevation extremes:

Lowest point: Drini i Bardhe/Beli Drim 297 m (located on the border with Albania)

Highest point: Gjeravica/Deravica 2,656 m

Natural resources: nickel, lead, zinc, magnesium, lignite, kaolin, chrome, bauxite

People ::Kosovo

Population: 1,815,048 (July 2010 est.)

Country comparison to the world: 148

Age structure:

0-14 years: 27.7% (male 260,678/female 239,779)

15-64 years: 65.7% (male 617,890/female 567,939)

65 years and over: 6.6% (male 50,463/female 68,089) (2010 est.)

Median age:

Total: 26.3 years

Male: 25.8 years

Female: 26.8 years (2010 est.)

Sex ratio:

At birth: 1.086 male(s)/female

Under 15 years: 1.09 male(s)/female

15-64 years: 1.09 male(s)/female

65 years and over: 0.74 male(s)/female

Total population: 1.06 male(s)/female (2010 est.)

Nationality:

Noun: Kosovar (Albanian), Kosovac (Serbian)

Adjective: Kosovar (Albanian), Kosovski (Serbian)

Note: Kosovan, a neutral term, is sometimes also used as a noun or adjective

Ethnic groups: Albanians 92%, other (Serb, Bosniak, Gorani, Roma, Turk, Ashkali, Egyptian) 8% (2008)

Religions: Muslim, Serbian Orthodox, Roman Catholic

Languages: Albanian (official), Serbian (official), Bosnian, Turkish, Roma

Literacy:

Definition: age 15 and over can read and write

Total population: 91.9%

Male: 96.6%

Female: 87.5% (2007 Census)

Government ::Kosovo

Country name:

Conventional long form: Republic of Kosovo

Conventional short form: Kosovo

Local long form: Republika e Kosoves (Republika Kosovo)

Local short form: Kosova (Kosovo)

Government type: republic

Capital:

Name: Pristina (Prishtine, Prishtina)

Geographic coordinates: 42 40 N, 21 10 E

Time difference: UTC+1 (6 hours ahead of Washington, DC during Standard Time)

Daylight saving time: +1hr, begins last Sunday in March; ends last Sunday in October

Administrative divisions: 30 municipalities (komunat, singular - komuna in Albanian; opstine, singular - opstina in Serbian); Decan (Decani), Dragash (Dragas), Ferizaj (Urosevac), Fushe Kosove (Kosovo Polje), Gjakove (Dakovica), Gjilan (Gnjilane), Gllogovc/Drenas (Glogovac), Istog (Istok), Kacanik, Kamenice/Dardana (Kamenica), Kline (Klina), Leposaviq (Leposavic), Lipjan (Lipljan), Malisheve (Malisevo), Mitrovice (Mitrovica),

Novoberde (Novo Brdo), Obiliq (Obilic), Peje (Pec), Podujeve (Podujevo), Prishtine (Pristina), Prizren, Rahovec (Orahovac), Shterpce (Strpce), Shtime (Stimlje), Skenderaj (Srbica), Suhareke (Suva Reka), Viti (Vitina), Vushtrri (Vucitrn), Zubin Potok, Zvecan note - the Government of Kosovo has announced the establishment of eight additional municipalities in accordance with UN Special Envoy AHTISAARI's mandated decentralization process; the boundaries of several municipalities are pending final approval; the

Municipalities are: Gracanice (Gracanica), Hani i Elezit (Dzeneral Jankovic), Junik, Kllokot-Verboc (Klokot-Vrbovac), Mamushe (Mamusa), Partes, and Ranillug (Ranilug); in addition, the current Mitrovice (Mitrovica) municipality is to be split into Mitrovice (Mitrovica) North and Mitrovice (Mitrovica) South

Independence: 17 February 2008 (from Serbia)

National holiday: Independence Day, 17 February (2008)

Constitution: adopted by the Kosovo Assembly on 9 April 2008; effective 15 June 2008

Legal system: evolving legal system based on terms of former UN Special Envoy Martti AHTISAARI's Plan for Kosovo's supervised independence; has not accepted compulsory ICJ jurisdiction

Suffrage: 18 years of age; universal

Executive branch:

Chief of state: Acting President Jakup KRASNIQI (since 27 September 2010)

Head of government: Prime Minister Hashim THACI (since 9 January 2008)

Cabinet: ministers; elected by the Kosovo Assembly (For more information visit the World Leaders website)

elections: the president elected for a five-year term by the Kosovo Assembly; election last held on 9 January 2008 (next to be held – a special election in 2011); the prime minister elected by the Kosovo Assembly

Election results: Fatmir SEJDIU reelected president after three rounds; note - resigned from the office of president on 27 Septermber 2010; Hashim THACI elected prime minister by the Assembly

Legislative branch: unicameral national Assembly (120 seats; 100 seats directly elected, 10 seats guaranteed for ethnic Serbs, 10 seats guaranteed for other ethnic minorities; members to serve four-year terms)

Elections: last held on 17 November 2007 (next expected to be held in 2011)

election results: percent of vote by party - PDK 34.3%, LDK 22.6%, AKR 12.3%, LDD 10.0%, AAK 9.6%, other 11.2%; seats by party – PDK 37, LDK 25, AKR 13, LDD 11, AAK 10, other 4

Judicial branch: Supreme Court; district courts; municipal courts

note: the Kosovo Constitution dictates that the Supreme Court of Kosovo is the highest judicial authority, and provides for a Kosovo Judicial Council (KJC) that proposes to the president candidates for ppointment or reappointment as judges and prosecutors; the KJC is also responsible for decisions on the promotion and transfer of judges and disciplinary proceedings against judges; at least 15 percent of Supreme Court and district court judges shall be from non-majority communities

Political parties and leaders: Albanian Christian Democratic Party of Kosovo or PShDK [Ton MARKU]; Alliance for a New Kosovo or AKR [Behgjet PACOLLI]; Alliance for the Future of Kosovo or AAK [Ramush HARADINAJ]; Alliance of Independent Social Democrats of Kosovo and Metohija or SDSKIM [Ljubisa ZIVIC]; Bosniak Vakat Coalition or DSV [Sadik IDRIZI]; Citizens' Initiative of Gora or GIG [Murselj HALJILJI]; Democratic Action Party or SDA [Numan BALIC]; Democratic League of Dardania or LDD [Nexhat DACI]; Democratic League of Kosovo or LDK [Fatmir SEJDIU]; Democratic Party of Ashkali of Kosovo or PDAK [Berat QERIMI]; Democratic Party of Bosniaks [Dzezair MURATI]; Democratic Party of Kosovo or PDK [Hashim THACI]; Independent Liberal Party or SLS [Slobadan PETROVIC]; Kosovo Democratic Turkish Party of KDTP [Mahir YAGCILAR]; New Democratic Initiative of Kosovo or IRDK [Xhevdet NEZIRAJ]; New Democratic Party or ND [Predrag JOVIC]; New Kosovo Alliance or AKR [Behxhet PACOLLI]; Reform Party Ora [Teuta SAHATCIA]; Serb National Party or SNS [Mihailo SCEPANOVIC]; Serbian Democratic Party of Kosovo and Metohija or SDS KiM [Slavisa PETKOVIC]; Serbian Kosovo and Metohija Party or SKMS [Dragisa MIRIC]; Serbian National Council of Northern Kosovo and Metohija or SNV [Milan IVANOVIC]; Social Democratic Party of Kosovo or PSDK [Agim CEKU]; Socialist Party of Kosovo or PSK [Emrush XHEMAJLI]; United Roma Party of Kosovo or PREBK [Haxhi Zylfi MERXHA]

Political pressure groups and leaders: Council for the Defense of Human Rights and Freedom (human rights); Humanitarian Law Centre (human rights); Movement for Self-Determination; Serb National Council (SNV)

International organization participation: IBRD, IDA, IFC, IMF, ITUC, MIGA

Diplomatic representation in the US:

Chief of mission: Ambassador Avni SPAHIU

Chancery: 1101 30th Street NW, Suites 330/340, Washington, DC 20007

Telephone: 202-380-3581

FAX: 202-380-3628

Consulate general: New York

Diplomatic representation from the US:

Chief of mission: Ambassador Christopher William DELL

Embassy: Arberia/Dragodan, Nazim Hikmet 30, Pristina, Kosovo

Mailing address: use embassy street address

Telephone: [381] 38 59 59 3000

FAX: [381] 38 549 890

Flag description: centered on a dark blue field is the geographical shape of Kosovo in a gold color surmounted by six white, five-pointed stars arrayed in a slight arc; each star represents one of the major ethnic groups of Kosovo: Albanians, Serbs, Turks, Gorani, Roma, and Bosniaks

National anthem:

Name: "Europe"

Lyrics/music: none/Mendi MENGJIQI

Note: adopted 2008; Kosovo chose to not include lyrics in its anthem so as not to offend minority ethnic groups in the country

Economy - overview: Over the past few years Kosovo's economy has shown significant progress in transitioning to a market-based system and maintaining macroeconomic stability, but it is still highly dependent on the international community and the diaspora for financial and technical assistance. Remittances from the diaspora - located mainly in Germany and Switzerland - are estimated to account for about 14% of GDP, and donor-financed activities and aid for another 7.5%. Kosovo's citizens are the poorest in Europe with an average annual per capita income of only $2,500. Unemployment, around 40% of the population, is a significant problem that encourages outward migration and black market activity. Most of Kosovo's population lives in rural towns outside of the capital, Pristina. Inefficient, near-subsistence farming is common - the result of small plots, limited mechanization, and lack of technical expertise. With international assistance, Kosovo has been able to privatize 50% of its state-owned enterprises (SOEs) by number, and over 90% of SOEs by value. Minerals and metals - including lignite, lead, zinc, nickel, chrome, aluminum, magnesium, and a wide variety of construction materials - once formed the backbone of industry, but output has declined because of ageing equipment and insufficient investment. A limited and unreliable electricity supply due to technical and financial problems is a major impediment to economic development. Kosovo's Ministry of Energy and Mining has solicited expressions of interest from private investors to develop a new power plant in order to address Kosovo and the region's unmet and growing demands for power. The official currency of Kosovo is the euro, but the Serbian dinar is also used in Serb enclaves. Kosovo's tie to the euro has helped keep core inflation low. Kosovo has one of the most open economies in the region, and continues to work with the international community on measures to improve the business environment and attract foreign investment. Kosovo has kept the government budget in balance as a result of efficient value added tax (VAT) collection at the borders and inefficient budget execution. In order to help integrate Kosovo into regional economic structures, UNMIK signed (on behalf of Kosovo) its accession to the Central Europe Free Trade Area (CEFTA) in 2006. However, Serbia and Bosnia have refused to recognize Kosovo's customs stamp or extend reduced tariff privileges for Kosovo products under CEFTA. In July 2008, Kosovo received pledges of $1.9 billion from 37 countries in support of its reform priorities. In June 2009, Kosovo joined the World Bank and International Monetary Fund, and Kosovo began servicing its share of the former Yugoslavia's debt.

GDP (purchasing power parity): $5.3 billion (2008); $4.7 billion

Country comparison to the world: 158

GDP (official exchange rate): $3.237 billion (2007 est.)

GDP - real growth rate:

GDP - per capita (PPP): $2,500 (2007)

Country comparison to the world: 174

GDP - composition by sector:

Agriculture: 12.9%

Industry: 22.6%

Services: 64.5% (2010 est.)

Labor force: NA (2009 est.)

Labor force - by occupation:

Agriculture: 16.5%

Industry: NA

Services: NA (2007 est.)

Unemployment rate: 16.6% (2009 est.); 14%

Country comparison to the world: 157

Population below poverty line: 35% (2007 est.)

Distribution of family income - Gini index: 30 (FY05/06)

Investment (gross fixed): 15.2% of GDP (2010 est.)

Country comparison to the world: 127

Public debt: NA% of GDP

Inflation rate (consumer prices): 5.3% (2007 est.)

Country comparison to the world: 150

Commercial bank prime lending rate: 14.09% (31 December 2009 est.)

Country comparison to the world: 55 13.79% (31 December 2008 est.)

Agriculture - products: wheat, corn, berries, potatoes, peppers

Industries: mineral mining, construction materials, base metals, leather, machinery, appliances

Electricity - production: 832 million kWh (2006)

Country comparison to the world: 149

Electricity - consumption: 4.281 billion kWh (2006)

Country comparison to the world: 115

Oil - production: 0 bbl/day (2007)

Country comparison to the world: 158

Oil - consumption: NA bbl/day

Oil - proved reserves: NA bbl

Natural gas - production: 0 cu m (2007)

Country comparison to the world: 169

Natural gas - consumption: 0 cu m (2007)

Country comparison to the world: 123

Natural gas - proved reserves: NA cu m

Current account balance: -$2.716 billion (2010 est.)

Country comparison to the world: 165 -$2.408 billion (2009 est.)

Exports: $527 million (2007 est.)

Exports - commodities: mining and processed metal products, scrap metals, leather products, machinery, appliances

Imports: $2.6 billion f.o.b. (2007 est.)

Imports - commodities: foodstuffs, wood, petroleum, chemicals, machinery and electrical equipment

Reserves of foreign exchange and gold: $NA

Debt - external: $NA

Stock of direct foreign investment - at home: $21.2 billion (31 December 2010 est.)

Country comparison to the world: 67$21.32 billion (31 December 2009 est.)

Exchange rates: euros (EUR) per US dollar - 0.7715 (2010), 0.7338 (2009), 0.6827 (2008), 0.7345 (2007)

Communications ::Kosovo

Telephones - main lines in use: 106,300 (2006)

Country comparison to the world: 143

Telephones - mobile cellular: 562,000 (2007)

Country comparison to the world: 157

Transportation ::Kosovo

Airports: 8 (2010)

Country comparison to the world: 165

Airports - with paved runways:

Total: 4

2,438 to 3,047 m: 1

1,524 to 2,437 m: 1

Under 914 m: 2 (2010)

Airports - with unpaved runways:

Total: 4

Under 914 m: 4 (2010)

Heliports: 2 (2010)

Railways:

Total: 430 km

Country comparison to the world: 116

Standard gauge: 430 km 1.435-m gauge (2007)

Roadways:

Total: 1,926 km

Country comparison to the world: 175

Paved: 1,668 km

Unpaved: 258 km (2009)

Military ::Kosovo

Military branches: Kosovo Security Force (2010)

Manpower fit for military service:

Males age 16-49: 429,645

Females age 16-49: 389,071 (2010 est.)

Disputes - international: Serbia with several other states protest
the US and other states' recognition of Kosovo's declaring itself as a
sovereign and independent state in February 2008; ethnic Serbian
municipalities along Kosovo's northern border challenge final status
of Kosovo-Serbia boundary; several thousand NATO-led KFOR
peacekeepers under UNMIK authority continue to keep the peace
within Kosovo between the ethnic Albanian majority and the Serb
minority in Kosovo; Kosovo and Macedonia completed demarcation
of their boundaryin September 2008

Refugees and internally displaced persons:

IDP's: 21,000 (2007)

Page last updated on January 12, 2011

REFER THIS INFORMATION BEFORE READING THIS BOOK

References

Guide to Country Profiles

These are the Categories, Fields, and subfields of information generally recorded for each country. Links are to the Definitions and Notes about each entry.

Introduction::

Background:

Geography::

Location:

Geographic coordinates:

Map references:

Area:

Total

Land

Water

Area - comparative:

Land boundaries:

Total

Border countries

Coastline:

Maritime claims:

Territorial sea

Contiguous zone

Exclusive economic zone

Continental shelf

Exclusive fishing zone

Climate:

Terrain:

Elevation extremes:

Lowest point

Highest point

Natural resources:

Land use:

Arable land

Permanent crops

Other

Irrigated land:

Total Renewable Water Resources:

Freshwater withdrawal (domestic/industrial/agricultural):

Total

Per capita

Natural hazards:

Volcanism

Environment - current issues:

Environment - international agreements:

Party to

Signed, but not ratified

Geography - note:

People::

Population:

Age structure:

0-14 years

15-64 years

65 years and over

Median Age:

Total

Male

Female

Population growth rate:

Birth rate:

Death rate:

Net migration rate:

Sex ratio:

At birth

Under 15 years

15-64 years

65 years and over

Total population

Infant mortality rate:

Total

Male

Female

Life expectancy at birth:

Total population

Male

Female

Total fertility rate:

HIV/AIDS - adult prevalence rate:

HIV/AIDS - people living with HIV/AIDS:

HIV/AIDS - deaths:

Major infectious diseases:

Degree of risk

Food or waterborne diseases

Vector borne diseases

Water contact diseases

Aerosolized dust or soil contact disease

Respiratory disease

Animal contact disease

Nationality:

Noun

Adjective

Ethnic groups:

Religions:

Languages:

Literacy:

Definition

Total population

Male

Female

School life expectancy (primary to tertiary):

Education expenditures:

People - note:

Government::

Country name:

Conventional long form

Conventional short form

Local long form

Local short form

Former

Abbreviation

Dependency status:

Government type:

Capital:

Name

Geographic coordinates

Time difference

Daylight saving time

Administrative divisions:

Dependent areas:

Independence:

National holiday:

Constitution:

Legal system:

Suffrage:

Executive branch:

Chief of state

Head of government

Cabinet

Elections

Election results

Legislative branch:

Elections

Election results

Judicial branch:

Political parties and leaders:

Political pressure groups and leaders:

International organization participation:

Diplomatic representation in the US:

Chief of mission

Chancery

Telephone

FAX

Consulate(s) general

Consulate(s)

Diplomatic representation from the US:

Chief of mission

Embassy

Mailing address

Telephone

FAX

Consulate(s) general

Consulate(s)

Branch office(s)

Flag description:

Government - note:

Economy:

Economy - overview:

GDP (purchasing power parity):

GDP (official exchange rate):

GDP - real growth rate:

GDP - per capita (PPP):

GDP - composition by sector:

Agriculture

Industry

Services

Labor force:

Labor force - by occupation:

Agriculture

Industry

Services

Unemployment rate:

Population below poverty line:

Household income or consumption by percentage share:

Lowest 10%

Highest 10%

Distribution of family income - Gini index:

Investment (gross fixed):

Budget:

Revenues

Expenditures

Public debt:

Inflation rate (consumer prices):

Central bank discount rate:

Commercial bank prime lending rate:

Stock of money:

Stock of quasi money:

Stock of domestic credit:

Market value of publicly traded shares:

Agriculture - products:

Industries:

Industrial production growth rate:

Electricity - production:

Electricity - consumption:

Electricity - exports:

Electricity - imports:

Oil - production:

Oil - consumption:

Oil - exports:

Oil - imports:

Oil - proved reserves:

Natural gas - production:

Natural gas - consumption:

Natural gas - exports:

Natural gas - imports:

Natural gas - proved reserves:

Current account balance:

Exports:

Exports - commodities:

Exports - partners:

Imports:

Imports - commodities:

Imports - partners:

Reserves of foreign exchange and gold:

Debt - external:

Stock of direct foreign investment - at home:

Stock of direct foreign investment - abroad:

Exchange rates:

Communications::

Telephones - main lines in use:

Telephones - mobile cellular:

Telephone system:

General assessment

Domestic

International

Broadcast media:

Internet country code:

Internet hosts:

Internet users:

Communications - note:

Transportation::

Airports:

Airports - with paved runways:

Total

Over 3,047 m

2,438 to 3,047 m

1,524 to 2,437 m

914 to 1,530 m

Under 914 m

Airports - with unpaved runways:

Total

Over 3,047 m

2,438 to 3,047 m

1,524 to 2,437 m

914 to 1,530 m

Under 914 m

Heliports:

Pipelines:

Railways:

Total

Broad gauge

Standard gauge

Narrow gauge

Dual gauge

Roadways:

Total

Paved

Unpaved

Waterways:

Merchant marine:

Total

Ships by type

Foreign-owned

Registered in other countries

Ports and terminals:

Transportation - note:

Military::

Military branches:

Military service age and obligation:

Manpower available for military service:

Males age 16-49

Females age 16-49

Manpower fit for military service:

Males age 16-49

Females age 16-49

Manpower reaching military age annually:

Males

Females

Military expenditures - percent of GDP:

Military - note:

Transnational Issues::

Disputes - international:

Refugees and internally displaced persons:

Refugees

IDPs

Trafficking in persons:

Current situation

Tier rating

Illicit drugs:

References:: Guide to Country Comparisons

Country Comparison pages are presorted lists of data from selected Factbook data fields. Country Comparison pages are generally given in descending order - highest to lowest - such as Population and Area. The two exceptions are Unemployment Rate and Inflation Rate, which are in ascending - lowest to highest - order. Country Comparison pages are available for the following 58 fields in six of the nine Factbook categories.

Geography::

Area:

Total

People::

Population:

Population growth rate:

Birth rate:

Death rate:

Net migration rate:

Infant mortality rate:

Life expectancy at birth:

Total fertility rate:

HIV/AIDS - adult prevalence rate:

HIV/AIDS - people living with HIV/AIDS:

HIV/AIDS - deaths:

Education expenditures:

Economy::

GDP (purchasing power parity):

GDP real growth rate:

GDP - per capita (PPP):

Labor force:

Unemployment rate:

Distribution of family income - Gini Index:

Investment (gross fixed):

Public debt:

Inflation rate (consumer prices):

Central bank discount rate:

Commercial bank prime lending rate:

Stock of money:

Stock of quasi money:

Stock of domestic credit:

Market value of publicly traded shares:

Industrial production growth rate:

Electricity - production:

Electricity - consumption:

Oil - production:

Oil - consumption:

Oil - exports:

Oil - imports:

Oil - proved reserves:

Natural gas - production:

Natural gas - consumption:

Natural gas - exports:

Natural gas - imports:

Natural gas - proved reserves:

Current account balance:

Exports:

Imports:

Reserves of foreign exchange and gold:

Debt - external:

Stock of direct foreign investment - at home:

Stock of direct foreign investment - abroad:

Communications::

Telephones - main lines in use:

Telephones - mobile cellular:

Internet hosts:

Internet users:

Transportation::

Airports:

Railways:

Total

Roadways:

Total

Waterways:

Merchant marine:

Total

Military::

Military expenditures - percent of GDP:

Not all Country Comparisons include the same number of entries because information for a particular field is not available for all countries. In addition, not all data fields are suitable for displaying as Country Comparisons, such as those containing textual information. Textual information is more readily viewed by clicking on the Field Listing icon next to the Data field title.

A

Abbreviations

This information is included in Appendix A: Abbreviations, which includes all abbreviations and acronyms used in the Factbook, with their expansions.

Acronyms

An acronym is an abbreviation coined from the initial letter of each successive word in a term or phrase. In general, an acronym made up solely from the first letter of the major words in the expanded form is rendered in all capital letters (NATO from North Atlantic Treaty Organization; an exception would be ASEAN for Association of Southeast Asian Nations). In general, an acronym made up of more than the first letter of the major words in the expanded form is rendered with only an initial capital letter (Comsat from Communications Satellite Corporation; an exception would be NAM from Nonaligned Movement). Hybrid forms are sometimes used to distinguish between initially identical terms (ICC for International Chamber of Commerce and ICCt for International Criminal Court).

Administrative divisions

This entry generally gives the numbers, designatory terms, and first-order administrative divisions as approved by the US Board on Geographic Names (BGN). Changes that have been reported but not yet acted on by the BGN are noted.

Age structure

This entry provides the distribution of the population according to age. Information is included by sex and age group (0-14 years, 15-64 years, 65 years and over). The age structure of a population affects a nation's key socioeconomic issues. Countries with young populations (high percentage under age 15) need to invest more in schools, while countries with older populations (high percentage ages 65 and over) need to invest more in the health sector. The age structure can also be used to help predict potential political issues. For example, the rapid growth of a young adult population unable to find employment can lead to unrest.

Agriculture - products

This entry is an ordered listing of major crops and products starting with the most important.

Airports

This entry gives the total number of airports or airfields recognizable from the air. The runway(s) may be paved (concrete or asphalt surfaces) or unpaved (grass, earth, sand, or gravel surfaces) and may include closed or abandoned installations. Airports or airfields that are no longer recognizable (overgrown, no facilities, etc.) are not included. Note that not all airports have accommodations for refueling, maintenance, or air traffic control.

Airports - with paved runways

This entry gives the total number of airports with paved runways (concrete or asphalt surfaces) by length. For airports with more than one runway, only the longest runway is included according to the following five groups - (1) over 3,047 m (over 10,000 ft), (2) 2,438 to 3,047 m (8,000 to 10,000 ft), (3) 1,524 to 2,437 m (5,000 to 8,000 ft), (4) 914 to 1,523 m (3,000 to 5,000 ft), and (5) under 914 m (under 3,000 ft). Only airports with usable runways are included in this listing. Not all airports have facilities for refueling, maintenance, or air traffic control. The type aircraft capable of operating from a runway of a given length is dependent upon a number of factors including elevation of the runway, runway gradient, average maximum daily temperature at the airport, engine types, flap settings, and take-off weight of the aircraft.

Airports - with unpaved runways

This entry gives the total number of airports with unpaved runways (grass, dirt, sand, or gravel surfaces) by length. For airports with more than one runway, only the longest runway is included according to the following five groups - (1) over 3,047 m (over 10,000 ft), (2) 2,438 to 3,047 m (8,000 to 10,000 ft), (3) 1,524 to 2,437 m (5,000 to 8,000 ft), (4) 914 to 1,523 m (3,000 to 5,000 ft), and (5) under 914 m (under 3,000 ft). Only airports with usable runways are included in this listing. Not all airports have facilities for refueling, maintenance, or air traffic control. The type aircraft capable of operating from a runway of a given length is dependent upon a number of factors including elevation of the runway, runway gradient, average maximum daily temperature at the airport, engine types, flap settings, and take-off weight of the aircraft.

Appendixes

This section includes Factbook-related material by topic.

Area

This entry includes three subfields. Total area is the sum of all land and water areas delimited by international boundaries and/or coastlines. Land area is the aggregate of all surfaces delimited by international boundaries and/or coastlines, excluding inland water bodies (lakes, reservoirs, rivers). Water area is the sum of the surfaces of all inland water bodies, such as lakes, reservoirs, or rivers, as delimited by international boundaries and/or coastlines.

Area - comparative

This entry provides an area comparison based on total area equivalents. Most entities are compared with the entire US or one of the 50 states based on area measurements (1990 revised) provided by the US Bureau of the Census. The smaller entities are compared with Washington, DC (178 sq km, 69 sq mi) or The Mall in Washington, DC (0.59 sq km, 0.23 sq mi, 146 acres).

B

Background

This entry usually highlights major historic events and current issues and may include a statement about one or two key future trends.

Birth rate

This entry gives the average annual number of births during a year per 1,000 persons in the population at midyear; also known as crude birth rate. The birth rate is usually the dominant factor in determining the rate of population growth. It depends on both the level of fertility and the age structure of the population.

Broadcast media

This entry provides information on the approximate number of public and private TV and radio stations in a country, as well as basic information on the availability of satellite and cable TV services.

Budget

This entry includes revenues, expenditures, and capital expenditures. These figures are calculated on an exchange rate basis, i.e., not in purchasing power parity (PPP) terms.

C

Capital

This entry gives the name of the seat of government, its geographic coordinates, the time difference relative to Coordinated Universal Time (UTC) and the time observed in Washington, DC, and, if applicable, information on daylight saving time (DST). Where appropriate, a special note has been added to highlight those countries that have multiple time zones.

Central bank discount rate

This entry provides the annualized interest rate a country's central bank charges commercial, depository banks for loans to meet temporary shortages of funds.

Climate

This entry includes a brief description of typical weather regimes throughout the year.

Coastline

This entry gives the total length of the boundary between the land area (including islands) and the sea.

Commercial bank prime lending rate

This entry provides a simple average of annualized interest rates commercial banks charge on new loans, denominated in the national currency, to their most credit-worthy customers.

Communications

This category deals with the means of exchanging information and includes the telephone, radio, television, and Internet host entries.

Communications - note

This entry includes miscellaneous communications information of significance not included elsewhere.

Constitution

This entry includes the dates of adoption, revisions, and major amendments.

Coordinated Universal Time (UTC)

UTC is the international atomic time scale that serves as the basis of timekeeping for most of the world. The hours, minutes, and seconds expressed by UTC represent the time of day at the Prime Meridian (0 deg. longitude) located near Greenwich, England as reckoned from midnight. UTC is calculated by the Bureau International des Poids et Measures (BIPM) in Sevres, France. The BIPM averages data collected from more than 200 atomic time and frequency standards located at about 50 laboratories worldwide. UTC is the basis for all civil time with the Earth divided into time zones expressed as positive or negative differences from UTC. UTC is also referred to as "Zulu time." See the Standard Time Zones of the World map included with the Reference Maps.

Country data codes

See Data codes.

Country map

Most versions of the Factbook provide a country map in color. The maps were produced from the best information available at the time of preparation. Names and/or boundaries may have changed subsequently.

Country name

This entry includes all forms of the country's name approved by the US Board on Geographic Names (Italy is used as an example): conventional long form (Italian Republic), conventional short form (Italy), local long form (Repubblica Italiana), local short form (Italia), former (Kingdom of Italy), as well as the abbreviation. Also see the Terminology note.

Crude oil

See entry for oil.

Current account balance

This entry records a country's net trade in goods and services, plus net earnings from rents, interest, profits, and dividends, and net transfer payments (such as pension funds and worker remittances) to and from the rest of the world during the period specified. These figures are calculated on an exchange rate basis, i.e., not in purchasing power parity (PPP) terms.

D

Data codes

This information is presented in This information is presented in <a href = "../appendix/appendix-d.html"Appendix D: Cross-Reference List of Country Data Codes and and <a href = "../appendix/appendix-e.html" Appendix E: Cross-Reference List of Hydrographic Data Codes.

Date of information

In general, information available as of January in a given year is used in the preparation of the printed edition.

Daylight Saving Time (DST)

This entry is included for those entities that have adopted a policy of adjusting the official local time forward, usually one hour, from Standard Time during summer months. Such policies are most common in mid-latitude regions.

Death rate

This entry gives the average annual number of deaths during a year per 1,000 population at midyear; also known as crude death rate. The death rate, while only a rough indicator of the mortality situation in a country, accurately indicates the current mortality impact on population growth. This indicator is significantly affected by age distribution, and most countries will eventually show a rise in the overall death rate, in spite of continued decline in mortality at all ages, as declining fertility results in an aging population.

Debt - external

This entry gives the total public and private debt owed to nonresidents repayable in internationally accepted currencies, goods, or services. These figures are calculated on an exchange rate basis, i.e., not in purchasing power parity (PPP) terms.

Dependency status

This entry describes the formal relationship between a particular nonindependent entity and an independent state.

Dependent areas

This entry contains an alphabetical listing of all nonindependent entities associated in some way with a particular independent state.

Diplomatic representation

The US Government has diplomatic relations with 189 independent states, including 187 of the 192 UN members (excluded UN members are Bhutan, Cuba, Iran, North Korea, and the US itself). In addition, the US has diplomatic relations with 2 independent states that are not in the UN, the Holy See and Kosovo, as well as with the EU.

Diplomatic representation from the US

This entry includes the chief of mission, embassy address, mailing address, telephone number, FAX number, branch office locations, consulate general locations, and consulate locations.

Diplomatic representation in the US

This entry includes the chief of mission, chancery, telephone, FAX, consulate general locations, and consulate locations.

Disputes - international

This entry includes a wide variety of situations that range from traditional bilateral boundary disputes to unilateral claims of one sort or another. Information regarding disputes over international terrestrial and maritime boundaries has been reviewed by the US Department of State. References to other situations involving borders or frontiers may also be included, such as resource disputes, geopolitical questions, or irredentist issues; however, inclusion does not necessarily constitute official acceptance or recognition by the US Government.

Distribution of family income - Gini index

This index measures the degree of inequality in the distribution of family income in a country. The index is calculated from the Lorenz curve, in which cumulative family income is plotted against the number of families arranged from the poorest to the richest. The index is the ratio of (a) the area between a country's Lorenz curve and the 45 degree helping line to (b) the entire triangular area under the 45 degree line. The more nearly equal a country's income distribution, the closer its Lorenz curve to the 45 degree line and the lower its Gini index, e.g., a Scandinavian country with an index of 25. The more unequal a country's income distribution, the farther its Lorenz curve from the 45 degree line and the higher its Gini index, e.g., a Sub-Saharan country with an index of 50. If income were distributed with perfect equality, the Lorenz curve would coincide with the 45 degree line and the index would be zero; if income were distributed with perfect inequality, the Lorenz curve would coincide with the horizontal axis and the right vertical axis and the index would be 100.

E

Economy

This category includes the entries dealing with the size, development, and management of productive resources, i.e., land, labor, and capital.

Economy - overview

This entry briefly describes the type of economy, including the degree of market orientation, the level of economic development, the most important natural resources, and the unique areas of specialization. It also characterizes major economic events and policy changes in the most recent 12 months and may include a statement about one or two key future macroeconomic trends.

Education expenditures

This entry provides the public expenditure on education as a percent of GDP.

Electricity - consumption

This entry consists of total electricity generated annually plus imports and minus exports, expressed in kilowatt-hours. The discrepancy between the amount of electricity generated and/or imported and the amount consumed and/or exported is accounted for as loss in transmission and distribution.

Electricity - exports

This entry is the total exported electricity in kilowatt-hours.

Electricity - imports

This entry is the total imported electricity in kilowatt-hours.

Electricity - production

This entry is the annual electricity generated expressed in kilowatt-hours. The discrepancy between the amount of electricity generated and/or imported and the amount consumed and/or exported is accounted for as loss in transmission and distribution.

Elevation extremes

This entry includes both the highest point and the lowest point.

Entities

Some of the independent states, dependencies, areas of special sovereignty, and governments included in this publication are not independent, and others are not officially recognized by the US Government. "Independent state" refers to a people politically organized into a sovereign state with a definite territory. "Dependencies" and "areas of special sovereignty" refer to a broad category of political entities that are associated in some way with an independent state. "Country" names used in the table of contents or for page headings are usually the short-form names as approved by the US Board on Geographic Names and may include independent states, dependencies, and areas of special sovereignty, or other geographic entities. There are a total of 266 separate geographic entities in The World Factbook that may be categorized as follows: INDEPENDENT STATES 194 Afghanistan, Albania, Algeria, Andorra, Angola, Antigua and Barbuda, Argentina, Armenia, Australia, Austria, Azerbaijan, The Bahamas, Bahrain, Bangladesh, Barbados, Belarus, Belgium, Belize, Benin, Bhutan, Bolivia, Bosnia and Herzegovina, Botswana, Brazil, Brunei, Bulgaria, Burkina Faso, Burma, Burundi, Cambodia, Cameroon, Canada, Cape Verde, Central African Republic, Chad, Chile, China, Colombia, Comoros, Democratic Republic of the Congo, Republic of the Congo, Costa Rica, Cote d'Ivoire, Croatia, Cuba, Cyprus, Czech Republic, Denmark, Djibouti, Dominica, Dominican Republic, Ecuador, Egypt, El Salvador, Equatorial Guinea,

Eritrea, Estonia, Ethiopia, Fiji, Finland, France, Gabon, The Gambia, Georgia, Germany, Ghana, Greece, Grenada, Guatemala, Guinea, Guinea-Bissau, Guyana, Haiti, Holy See, Honduras, Hungary, Iceland, India, Indonesia, Iran, Iraq, Ireland, Israel, Italy, Jamaica, Japan, Jordan, Kazakhstan, Kenya, Kiribati, North Korea, South Korea, Kosovo, Kuwait, Kyrgyzstan, Laos, Latvia, Lebanon, Lesotho, Liberia, Libya, Liechtenstein, Lithuania, Luxembourg, Macedonia, Madagascar, Malawi, Malaysia, Maldives, Mali, Malta, Marshall Islands, Mauritania, Mauritius, Mexico, Federated States of Micronesia, Moldova, Monaco, Mongolia, Montenegro, Morocco, Mozambique, Namibia, Nauru, Nepal, Netherlands, NZ, Nicaragua, Niger, Nigeria, Norway, Oman, Pakistan, Palau, Panama, Papua New Guinea, Paraguay, Peru, Philippines, Poland, Portugal, Qatar, Romania, Russia, Rwanda, Saint Kitts and Nevis, Saint Lucia, Saint Vincent and the Grenadines, Samoa, San Marino, Sao Tome and Principe, Saudi Arabia, Senegal, Serbia, Seychelles, Sierra Leone, Singapore, Slovakia, Slovenia, Solomon Islands, Somalia, South Africa, Spain, Sri Lanka, Sudan, Suriname, Swaziland, Sweden, Switzerland, Syria, Tajikistan, Tanzania, Thailand, Timor-Leste, Togo, Tonga, Trinidad and Tobago, Tunisia, Turkey, Turkmenistan, Tuvalu, Uganda, Ukraine, UAE, UK, US, Uruguay, Uzbekistan, Vanuatu, Venezuela, Vietnam, Yemen, Zambia, Zimbabwe OTHER 2 Taiwan, European Union DEPENDENCIES AND AREAS OF SPECIAL SOVEREIGNTY 6 Australia - Ashmore and Cartier Islands, Christmas Island, Cocos (Keeling) Islands, Coral Sea Islands, Heard Island and McDonald Islands, Norfolk Island 2 China - Hong Kong, Macau 2 Denmark - Faroe Islands, Greenland 9 France - Clipperton Island, French Polynesia, French Southern and Antarctic Lands, Mayotte, New Caledonia, Saint Barthelemy, Saint Martin, Saint Pierre and Miquelon, Wallis and Futuna 3 Netherlands - Aruba, Curacao, Sint Maarten 3 New Zealand - Cook Islands, Niue, Tokelau 3 Norway - Bouvet Island, Jan Mayen, Svalbard 17 UK - Akrotiri, Anguilla, Bermuda, British Indian Ocean Territory, British Virgin Islands, Cayman Islands, Dhekelia, Falkland Islands, Gibraltar, Guernsey, Jersey, Isle of Man, Montserrat, Pitcairn Islands, Saint Helena, South Georgia and the South Sandwich Islands, Turks and Caicos Islands 14 US - American Samoa, Baker Island*, Guam,

Howland Island*, Jarvis Island*, Johnston Atoll*, Kingman Reef*, Midway Islands*, Navassa Island, Northern Mariana Islands, Palmyra Atoll*, Puerto Rico, Virgin Islands, Wake Island (* consolidated in United States Pacific Island Wildlife Refuges entry) MISCELLANEOUS 6 Antarctica, Gaza Strip, Paracel Islands, Spratly Islands, West Bank, Western Sahara OTHER ENTITIES 5 oceans - Arctic Ocean, Atlantic Ocean, Indian Ocean, Pacific Ocean, Southern Ocean 1 World

267 total

Environment - current issues

This entry lists the most pressing and important environmental problems. The following terms and abbreviations are used throughout the entry: Acidification - the lowering of soil and water pH due to acid precipitation and deposition usually through precipitation; this process disrupts ecosystem nutrient flows and may kill freshwater fish and plants dependent on more neutral or alkaline conditions (see acid rain). Acid rain - characterized as containing harmful levels of sulfur dioxide or nitrogen oxide; acid rain is damaging and potentially deadly to the earth's fragile ecosystems; acidity is measured using the pH scale where 7 is neutral, values greater than 7 are considered alkaline, and values below 5.6 are considered acid precipitation; note - a pH of 2.4 (the acidity of vinegar) has been measured in rainfall in New England. Aerosol - a collection of airborne particles dispersed in a gas, smoke, or fog. Afforestation - converting a bare or agricultural space by planting trees and plants; reforestation involves replanting trees on areas that have been cut or destroyed by fire. Asbestos - a naturally occurring soft fibrous mineral commonly used in fireproofing materials and considered to be highly carcinogenic in particulate form. Biodiversity - also biological diversity; the relative number of species, diverse in form and function, at the genetic, organism, community, and ecosystem level; loss of biodiversity reduces an ecosystem's ability to recover from natural or man-induced disruption. Bio-indicators - a plant or animal species whose presence, abundance, and health reveal the general condition of its habitat. Biomass - the total weight or volume of living matter in a given area or volume. Carbon cycle - the term used to describe the exchange of carbon (in various forms, e.g., as carbon dioxide) between the atmosphere, ocean, terrestrial biosphere, and geological deposits. Catchments - assemblages used to capture and retain rainwater and runoff; an important water management technique in areas with limited freshwater resources, such as Gibraltar. DDT (dichloro-diphenyl-trichloro-ethane) - a colorless, odorless insecticide that has toxic effects on most animals; the use of DDT was banned in the US in 1972. Defoliants - chemicals which cause plants to lose their leaves artificially; often used in agricultural practices for weed control, and may have detrimental impacts on human and ecosystem health. Deforestation - the destruction of vast areas of forest (e.g., unsustainable forestry practices, agricultural and range land clearing, and the over exploitation of wood products for use as fuel) without planting new growth. Desertification - the spread of desert-like conditions in arid or semi-arid areas, due to overgrazing, loss of agriculturally productive soils, or climate change. Dredging - the practice of deepening an existing waterway; also, a technique used for collecting bottom-dwelling marine organisms (e.g., shellfish) or harvesting coral, often causing significant destruction of reef and ocean-floor ecosystems. Drift-net fishing - done with a net, miles in extent, that is generally anchored to a boat and left to float with the tide; often results in an over harvesting and waste of large populations of non-commercial marine species (by-catch) by its effect of "sweeping the ocean clean." Ecosystems - ecological units comprised of complex communities of organisms and their specific environments. Effluents - waste materials, such as smoke, sewage, or industrial waste which are released into the environment, subsequently polluting it. Endangered species - a species that is threatened with extinction either by direct hunting or habitat destruction. Freshwater - water with very low soluble mineral content; sources include lakes, streams, rivers, glaciers, and underground aquifers. Greenhouse gas - a gas that "traps" infrared radiation in the lower atmosphere causing surface warming; water vapor, carbon dioxide, nitrous oxide, methane, hydrofluorocarbons, and ozone are the primary greenhouse gases in the Earth's atmosphere. Groundwater -

water sources found below the surface of the earth often in naturally occurring reservoirs in permeable rock strata; the source for wells and natural springs. Highlands Water Project - a series of dams constructed jointly by Lesotho and South Africa to redirect Lesotho's abundant water supply into a rapidly growing area in South Africa; while it is the largest infrastructure project in southern Africa, it is also the most costly and controversial; objections to the project include claims that it forces people from their homes, submerges farmlands, and squanders economic resources. Inuit Circumpolar Conference (ICC) - represents the roughly 150,000 Inuits of Alaska, Canada, Greenland, and Russia in international environmental issues; a General Assembly convenes every three years to determine the focus of the ICC; the most current concerns are long-range transport of pollutants, sustainable development, and climate change. Metallurgical plants - industries which specialize in the science, technology, and processing of metals; these plants produce highly concentrated and toxic wastes which can contribute to pollution of ground water and air when not properly disposed. Noxious substances - injurious, very harmful to living beings. Overgrazing - the grazing of animals on plant material faster than it can naturally regrow leading to the permanent loss of plant cover, a common effect of too many animals grazing limited range land. Ozone shield - a layer of the atmosphere composed of ozone gas (O_3) that resides approximately 25 miles above the Earth's surface and absorbs solar ultraviolet radiation that can be harmful to living organisms. Poaching - the illegal killing of animals or fish, a great concern with respect to endangered or threatened species. Pollution - the contamination of a healthy environment by man-made waste. Potable water - water that is drinkable, safe to be consumed. Salination - the process through which fresh (drinkable) water becomes salt (undrinkable) water; hence, desalination is the reverse process; also involves the accumulation of salts in topsoil caused by evaporation of excessive irrigation water, a process that can eventually render soil incapable of supporting crops. Siltation - occurs when water channels and reservoirs become clotted with silt and mud, a side effect of deforestation and soil erosion. Slash-and-burn agriculture - a rotating cultivation technique in which trees are cut down and burned in order to clear land for temporary agriculture; the land is used until its productivity declines at which point a new plot is selected and the process repeats; this practice is sustainable while population levels are low and time is permitted for regrowth of natural vegetation; conversely, where these conditions do not exist, the practice can have disastrous consequences for the environment. Soil degradation - damage to the land's productive capacity because of poor agricultural practices such as the excessive use of pesticides or fertilizers, soil compaction from heavy equipment, or erosion of topsoil, eventually resulting in reduced ability to produce agricultural products. Soil erosion - the removal of soil by the action of water or wind, compounded by poor agricultural practices, deforestation, overgrazing, and desertification. Ultraviolet (UV) radiation - a portion of the electromagnetic energy emitted by the sun and naturally filtered in the upper atmosphere by the ozone layer; UV radiation can be harmful to living organisms and has been linked to increasing rates of skin cancer in humans. Waterborne diseases - those in which bacteria survive in, and are transmitted through, water; always a serious threat in areas with an untreated water supply.

Environment - international agreements

This entry separates country participation in international environmental agreements into two levels - party to and signed, but not ratified. Agreements are listed in alphabetical order by the abbreviated form of the full name.

Environmental agreements

This information is presented in This information is presented in <a href = "../appendix/appendix-c.html"Appendix C: Selected International Environmental Agreements, which includes the name, abbreviation, date opened for signature, date entered into force, objective, and parties by category.

Ethnic groups

This entry provides an ordered listing of ethnic groups starting with the largest and normally includes the percent of total population.

Exchange rates

This entry provides the official value of a country's monetary unit at a given date or over a given period of time, as expressed in units of local currency per US dollar and as determined by international market forces or official fiat. The International Organization for Standardization (ISO) 4217 alphabetic currency code for the national medium of exchange is presented in parenthesis.

Executive branch

This entry includes several subfields. Chief of state includes the name and title of the titular leader of the country who represents the state at official and ceremonial functions but may not be involved with the day-to-day activities of the government. Head of government includes the name and title of the top administrative leader who is designated to manage the day-to-day activities of the government. For example, in the UK, the monarch is the chief of state, and the prime minister is the head of government. In the US, the president is both the chief of state and the head of government. Cabinet includes the official name for this body of high-ranking advisers and the method for selection of members. Elections includes the nature of election process or accession to power, date of the last election, and date of the next election. Election results includes the percent of vote for each candidate in the last election.

Exports

This entry provides the total US dollar amount of merchandise exports on an f.o.b. (free on board) basis. These figures are calculated on an exchange rate basis, i.e., not in purchasing power parity (PPP) terms.

Exports - commodities

This entry provides a listing of the highest-valued exported products; it sometimes includes the percent of total dollar value.

Exports - partners

This entry provides a rank ordering of trading partners starting with the most important; it sometimes includes the percent of total dollar value.

F

Flag description

This entry provides a written flag description produced from actual flags or the best information available at the time the entry was written. The flags of independent states are used by their dependencies unless there is an officially recognized local flag. Some disputed and other areas do not have flags.

Flag graphic

Most versions of the Factbook include a color flag at the beginning of the country profile. The flag graphics were produced from actual flags or the best information available at the time of preparation. The flags of independent states are used by their dependencies unless there is an officially recognized local flag. Some disputed and other areas do not have flags.

Freshwater withdrawal (domestic/industrial/agricultural)

This entry provides the annual quantity of water in cubic kilometers removed from available sources for use in any purpose. Water drawn-off is not necessarily entirely consumed and some portion may be returned for further use downstream. Domestic sector use refers to water supplied by public distribution systems. Note that some of this total may be used for small industrial and/or limited agricultural purposes. Industrial sector use is the quantity of water used by self-supplied industries not connected to a public distribution system. Agricultural sector use includes water used for irrigation and livestock watering, and does not account for agriculture directly dependent on rainfall. Included are figures for total annual water withdrawal and per capita water withdrawal.

G

GDP (official exchange rate)

This entry gives the gross domestic product (GDP) or value of all final goods and services produced within a nation in a given year. A nation's GDP at official exchange rates (OER) is the home-currency-denominated annual GDP figure divided by the bilateral average US exchange rate with that country in that year. The measure is simple to compute and gives a precise measure of the value of output. Many economists prefer this measure when gauging the economic power an economy maintains vis-a-vis its neighbors, judging that an exchange rate captures the purchasing power a nation enjoys in the international marketplace. Official exchange rates, however, can be artificially fixed and/or subject to manipulation - resulting in claims of the country having an under- or over-valued currency - and are not necessarily the equivalent of a market-determined exchange rate. Moreover, even if the official exchange rate is market-determined, market exchange rates are frequently established by a relatively small set of goods and services (the ones the country trades) and may not capture the value of the larger set of goods the country produces. Furthermore, OER-converted GDP is not well suited to comparing domestic GDP over time, since appreciation/depreciation from one year to the next will make the OER GDP value rise/fall regardless of whether home-currency-denominated GDP changed.

GDP (purchasing power parity)

This entry gives the gross domestic product (GDP) or value of all final goods and services produced within a nation in a given year. A nation's GDP at purchasing power parity (PPP) exchange rates is the sum value of all goods and services produced in the country valued at prices prevailing in the United States. This is the measure most economists prefer when looking at per-capita welfare and when comparing living conditions or use of resources across countries. The measure is difficult to compute, as a US dollar value has to be assigned to all goods and services in the country regardless of whether these goods and services have a direct equivalent in the United States (for example, the value of an ox-cart or non-US military equipment); as a result, PPP estimates for some countries are based on a small and sometimes different set of goods and services. In addition, many countries do not formally participate in the World Bank's PPP project that calculates these measures, so the resulting GDP estimates for these countries may lack precision. For many developing countries, PPP-based GDP measures are multiples of the official exchange rate (OER) measure. The differences between the OER- and PPP-denominated GDP values for most of the wealthy industrialized countries are generally much smaller.

GDP - composition by sector

This entry gives the percentage contribution of agriculture, industry, and services to total GDP. The distribution will total less than 100 percent if the data are incomplete.

GDP - per capita (PPP)

This entry shows GDP on a purchasing power parity basis divided by population as of 1 July for the same year.

GDP - real growth rate

This entry gives GDP growth on an annual basis adjusted for inflation and expressed as a percent.

GDP methodology

In the Economy category, GDP dollar estimates for countries are reported both on an official exchange rate (OER) and a purchasing power parity (PPP) basis. Both measures contain information that is useful to the reader. The PPP method involves the use of standardized international dollar price weights, which are applied to the quantities of final goods and services produced in a given economy. The data derived from the PPP method probably provide the best available starting point for comparisons of economic strength and well-being between countries. In contrast, the currency exchange rate method involves a variety of international and domestic financial forces that may not capture the value of domestic output. Whereas PPP estimates for OECD countries are quite reliable, PPP estimates for developing countries are often rough approximations. In developing countries with weak currencies, the exchange rate estimate of GDP in dollars is typically one-fourth to one-half the PPP estimate. Most of the GDP estimates for developing countries are based on extrapolation of PPP numbers published by the UN International Comparison Program (UNICP) and by Professors Robert Summers and Alan Heston of the University of Pennsylvania and their colleagues. GDP derived using the OER method should be used for the purpose of calculating the share of items such as exports, imports, military expenditures, external debt, or the current account balance, because the dollar values presented in the Factbook for these items have been converted at official exchange rates, not at PPP. One should use the OER GDP figure to calculate the proportion of, say, Chinese defense expenditures in GDP, because that share will be the same as one calculated in local currency units. Comparison of OER GDP with PPP GDP may also indicate whether a currency is over- or under-valued. If OER GDP is smaller than PPP GDP, the official exchange rate may be undervalued, and vice versa. However, there is no strong historical evidence that market exchange rates move in the direction implied by the PPP rate, at least not in the short- or medium-term. Note: the numbers for GDP and other economic data should not be chained together from successive volumes of the Factbook because of changes in the US dollar measuring rod, revisions of data by statistical agencies, use of new or different sources of information, and changes in national statistical methods and practices.

Geographic coordinates

This entry includes rounded latitude and longitude figures for the purpose of finding the approximate geographic center of an entity and is based on the locations provided in the Geographic Names Server

(GNS), maintained by the National Geospatial-Intelligence Agency on behalf of the US Board on Geographic Names.

Geographic names

This information is presented in This information is presented in <a href = "../appendix/appendix-f.html"Appendix F: Cross Reference List of Geographic Names. It includes a listing of various alternate names, former names, local names, and regional names referenced to one or more related Factbook entries. Spellings are normally, but not always, those approved by the US Board on Geographic Names (BGN). Alternate names and additional information are included in parentheses.

Geography

This category includes the entries dealing with the natural environment and the effects of human activity.

Geography - note

This entry includes miscellaneous geographic information of significance not included elsewhere.

Gini index

See entry for Distribution of family income - Gini index

GNP

Gross national product (GNP) is the value of all final goods and services produced within a nation in a given year, plus income earned by its citizens abroad, minus income earned by foreigners from domestic production. The Factbook, following current practice, uses GDP rather than GNP to measure national production. However, the user must realize that in certain countries net remittances from citizens working abroad may be important to national well-being.

Government

This category includes the entries dealing with the system for the adoption and administration of public policy.

Government - note

This entry includes miscellaneous government information of significance not included elsewhere.

Government type

This entry gives the basic form of government. Definitions of the major governmental terms are as follows. (Note that for some countries more than one definition applies.): Absolute monarchy - a form of government where the monarch rules unhindered, i.e., without any laws, constitution, or legally organized opposition. Anarchy - a condition of lawlessness or political disorder brought about by the absence of governmental authority. Authoritarian - a form of government in which state authority is imposed onto many aspects of citizens' lives. Commonwealth - a nation, state, or other political entity founded on law and united by a compact of the people for the common good. Communist - a system of government in which the state plans and controls the economy and a single - often authoritarian - party holds power; state controls are imposed with the elimination of private ownership of property or capital while claiming to make progress toward a higher social order in which all goods are equally shared by the people (i.e., a classless society). Confederacy (Confederation) - a union by compact or treaty between states, provinces, or territories, that creates a central government with limited powers; the constituent entities retain supreme authority over all matters except those delegated to the central government. Constitutional - a government by or operating under an authoritative document (constitution) that sets forth the system of fundamental laws and principles that determines the nature, functions, and limits of that government. Constitutional democracy - a form of government in which the sovereign power of the people is spelled out in a governing constitution. Constitutional monarchy - a system of government in which a monarch is guided by a constitution whereby his/her rights, duties, and responsibilities are spelled out in written law or by custom. Democracy - a form of government in which the supreme power is retained by the people, but which is usually exercised indirectly through a system of representation and delegated authority periodically renewed. Democratic republic - a state in which the supreme power rests in the body of citizens entitled to vote for officers and representatives responsible to them. Dictatorship - a form of government in which a ruler or small clique wield absolute power (not restricted by a constitution or laws). Ecclesiastical - a government administrated by a church. Emirate - similar to a monarchy or sultanate, but a government in which the supreme power is in the hands of an emir (the ruler of a Muslim state); the emir may be an absolute overlord or a sovereign with constitutionally limited authority. Federal (Federation) - a form of government in which sovereign power is formally divided - usually by means of a constitution - between a central authority and a number of constituent regions (states, colonies, or provinces) so that each region retains some management of its internal affairs; differs from a confederacy in that the central government exerts influence directly upon both individuals as well as upon the regional units. Federal republic - a state in which the powers of the central government are restricted and in which the component parts (states, colonies, or provinces) retain a degree of self-government; ultimate sovereign power rests with the voters who chose their governmental representatives. Islamic republic - a particular form of government adopted by some Muslim states; although such a state is, in theory, a theocracy, it remains a republic, but its laws are required to be compatible with the laws of Islam. Maoism - the theory and practice of Marxism-Leninism developed in China by Mao Zedong (Mao Tse-tung), which states that a continuous revolution is necessary if the leaders of a communist state are to keep in touch with the people. Marxism - the political, economic, and social principles espoused by 19th century economist Karl Marx; he viewed the struggle of workers as a progression of historical forces that would proceed from a class struggle of the proletariat (workers) exploited by capitalists (business owners), to a socialist "dictatorship of the proletariat," to, finally, a classless society - Communism. Marxism-Leninism - an expanded form of communism developed by Lenin from doctrines of Karl Marx; Lenin saw imperialism as the final stage of capitalism and shifted the focus of workers' struggle from developed to underdeveloped countries. Monarchy - a government in which the supreme power is lodged in the hands of a monarch who reigns over a state or territory, usually for life and by hereditary right; the monarch may be either a sole absolute ruler or a sovereign - such as a king, queen, or prince - with constitutionally limited authority. Oligarchy - a government in which control is exercised by a small group of individuals whose authority generally is based on wealth or power. Parliamentary democracy - a political system in which the legislature (parliament) selects the government - a prime minister, premier, or chancellor along with the cabinet ministers - according to party strength as expressed in elections; by this system, the government acquires a dual responsibility: to the people as well as to the parliament. Parliamentary government (Cabinet-Parliamentary government) - a government in which members of an executive branch (the cabinet and its leader - a prime minister, premier, or chancellor) are nominated to their positions by a legislature or parliament, and are directly responsible to it; this type of government can be dissolved at will by the parliament (legislature) by means of a no confidence vote or the leader of the cabinet may dissolve the parliament if it can no longer function. Parliamentary monarchy - a state headed by a monarch who is not actively involved in policy formation or implementation (i.e., the exercise of sovereign powers by a monarch in a ceremonial capacity); true governmental leadership is carried out by a cabinet and its head - a prime minister, premier, or chancellor - who are drawn from a legislature (parliament). Presidential - a system of government where the executive branch exists separately from a legislature (to which it is generally not accountable). Republic - a representative democracy in which the people's elected deputies (representatives), not the people themselves, vote on legislation.

Socialism - a government in which the means of planning, producing, and distributing goods is controlled by a central government that theoretically seeks a more just and equitable distribution of property and labor; in actuality, most socialist governments have ended up being no more than dictatorships over workers by a ruling elite. Sultanate - similar to a monarchy, but a government in which the supreme power is in the hands of a sultan (the head of a Muslim state); the sultan may be an absolute ruler or a sovereign with constitutionally limited authority. Theocracy - a form of government in which a Deity is recognized as the supreme civil ruler, but the Deity's laws are interpreted by ecclesiastical authorities (bishops, mullahs, etc.); a government subject to religious authority. Totalitarian - a government that seeks to subordinate the individual to the state by controlling not only all political and economic matters, but also the attitudes, values, and beliefs of its population.

Greenwich Mean Time (GMT)

The mean solar time at the Greenwich Meridian, Greenwich, England, with the hours and days, since 1925, reckoned from midnight. GMT is now a historical term having been replaced by UTC on 1 January 1972. See Coordinated Universal Time.

Gross domestic product

See GDP

Gross national product

See GNP

Gross world product

See GWP

GWP

This entry gives the gross world product (GWP) or aggregate value of all final goods and services produced worldwide in a given year.

H

Heliports

This entry gives the total number of heliports with hard-surface runways, helipads, or landing areas that support routine sustained helicopter operations exclusively and have support facilities including one or more of the following facilities: lighting, fuel, passenger handling, or maintenance. It includes former airports used exclusively for helicopter operations but excludes heliports limited to day operations and natural clearings that could support helicopter landings and takeoffs.

HIV/AIDS - adult prevalence rate

This entry gives an estimate of the percentage of adults (aged 15-49) living with HIV/AIDS. The adult prevalence rate is calculated by dividing the estimated number of adults living with HIV/AIDS at yearend by the total adult population at yearend.

HIV/AIDS - deaths

This entry gives an estimate of the number of adults and children who died of AIDS during a given calendar year.

HIV/AIDS - people living with HIV/AIDS

This entry gives an estimate of all people (adults and children) alive at yearend with HIV infection, whether or not they have developed symptoms of AIDS.

Household income or consumption by percentage share

Data on household income or consumption come from household surveys, the results adjusted for household size. Nations use different standards and procedures in collecting and adjusting the data. Surveys based on income will normally show a more unequal distribution than surveys based on consumption. The quality of surveys is improving with time, yet caution is still necessary in making inter-country comparisons.

Hydrographic data codes

See Data codes

I

Illicit drugs

This entry gives information on the five categories of illicit drugs - narcotics, stimulants, depressants (sedatives), hallucinogens, and cannabis. These categories include many drugs legally produced and prescribed by doctors as well as those illegally produced and sold outside of medical channels. Cannabis (Cannabis sativa) is the common hemp plant, which provides hallucinogens with some sedative properties, and includes marijuana (pot, Acapulco gold, grass, reefer), tetrahydrocannabinol (THC, Marinol), hashish (hash), and hashish oil (hash oil). Coca (mostly Erythroxylum coca) is a bush with leaves that contain the stimulant used to make cocaine. Coca is not to be confused with cocoa, which comes from cacao seeds and is used in making chocolate, cocoa, and cocoa butter. Cocaine is a stimulant derived from the leaves of the coca bush. Depressants (sedatives) are drugs that reduce tension and anxiety and include chloral hydrate, barbiturates (Amytal, Nembutal, Seconal, phenobarbital), benzodiazepines (Librium, Valium), methaqualone (Quaalude), glutethimide (Doriden), and others (Equanil, Placidyl, Valmid). Drugs are any chemical substances that effect a physical, mental, emotional, or behavioral change in an individual. Drug abuse is the use of any licit or illicit chemical substance that results in physical, mental, emotional, or behavioral impairment in an individual. Hallucinogens are drugs that affect sensation, thinking, self-awareness, and emotion. Hallucinogens include LSD (acid, microdot), mescaline and peyote (mexc, buttons, cactus), amphetamine variants (PMA, STP, DOB), phencyclidine (PCP, angel dust, hog), phencyclidine analogues (PCE, PCPy, TCP), and others (psilocybin, psilocyn). Hashish is the resinous exudate of the cannabis or hemp plant (Cannabis sativa). Heroin is a semisynthetic derivative of morphine. Mandrax is a trade name for methaqualone, a pharmaceutical depressant. Marijuana is the dried leaf of the cannabis or hemp plant (Cannabis sativa). Methaqualone is a pharmaceutical depressant, referred to as mandrax in Southwest Asia and Africa. Narcotics are drugs that relieve pain, often induce sleep, and refer to opium, opium derivatives, and synthetic substitutes. Natural narcotics include opium (paregoric, parepectolin), morphine (MS-Contin, Roxanol), codeine (Tylenol with codeine, Empirin with codeine, Robitussin AC), and thebaine. Semisynthetic narcotics include heroin (horse, smack), and hydromorphone (Dilaudid). Synthetic narcotics include meperidine or Pethidine (Demerol, Mepergan), methadone (Dolophine, Methadose), and others (Darvon, Lomotil). Opium is the brown, gummy exudate of the incised, unripe seedpod of the opium poppy. Opium poppy (Papaver somniferum) is the source for the natural and semisynthetic narcotics. Poppy straw is the entire cut and dried opium poppy-plant material, other than the seeds. Opium is extracted from poppy straw in commercial operations that produce the drug for medical use. Qat (kat, khat) is a stimulant from the buds or leaves of Catha edulis that is chewed or drunk as tea. Quaaludes is the North American slang term for methaqualone, a pharmaceutical depressant. Stimulants are drugs that relieve mild depression, increase energy and activity, and include cocaine (coke, snow, crack), amphetamines (Desoxyn, Dexedrine), ephedrine, ecstasy (clarity, essence, doctor, Adam), phenmetrazine (Preludin), methylphenidate (Ritalin), and others (Cylert, Sanorex, Tenuate).

Imports

This entry provides the total US dollar amount of merchandise imports on a c.i.f. (cost, insurance, and freight) or f.o.b. (free on board) basis. These figures are calculated on an exchange rate basis, i.e., not in purchasing power parity (PPP) terms.

Imports - commodities

This entry provides a listing of the highest-valued imported products; it sometimes includes the percent of total dollar value.

Imports - partners

This entry provides a rank ordering of trading partners starting with the most important; it sometimes includes the percent of total dollar value.

Independence

For most countries, this entry gives the date that sovereignty was achieved and from which nation, empire, or trusteeship. For the other countries, the date given may not represent "independence" in the strict sense, but rather some significant nationhood event such as the traditional founding date or the date of unification, federation, confederation, establishment, fundamental change in the form of government, or state succession. For a number of countries, the establishment of statehood was a lengthy evolutionary process occurring over decades or even centuries. In such cases, several significant dates are cited. Dependent areas include the notation "none" followed by the nature of their dependency status. Also see the Terminology note.

Industrial production growth rate

This entry gives the annual percentage increase in industrial production (includes manufacturing, mining, and construction).

Industries

This entry provides a rank ordering of industries starting with the largest by value of annual output.

Infant mortality rate

This entry gives the number of deaths of infants under one year old in a given year per 1,000 live births in the same year; included is the total death rate, and deaths by sex, male and female. This rate is often used as an indicator of the level of health in a country.

Inflation rate (consumer prices)

This entry furnishes the annual percent change in consumer prices compared with the previous year's consumer prices.

International disputes

see Disputes - international

International organization participation

This entry lists in alphabetical order by abbreviation those international organizations in which the subject country is a member or participates in some other way.

International organizations

This information is presented in This information is presented in <a href = "../appendix/appendix-b.html"Appendix B: International Organizations and Groups which includes the name, abbreviation, date established, aim, and members by category.

Internet country code

This entry includes the two-letter codes maintained by the International Organization for Standardization (ISO) in the ISO 3166 Alpha-2 list and used by the Internet Assigned Numbers Authority (IANA) to establish country-coded top-level domains (ccTLDs).

Internet hosts

This entry lists the number of Internet hosts available within a country. An Internet host is a computer connected directly to the Internet; normally an Internet Service Provider's (ISP) computer is a host. Internet users may use either a hard-wired terminal, at an institution with a mainframe computer connected directly to the Internet, or may connect remotely by way of a modem via telephone line, cable, or satellite to the Internet Service Provider's host computer. The number of hosts is one indicator of the extent of Internet connectivity.

Internet users

This entry gives the number of users within a country that access the Internet. Statistics vary from country to country and may include users who access the Internet at least several times a week to those who access it only once within a period of several months.

Introduction

This category includes one entry, Background.

Investment (gross fixed)

This entry records total business spending on fixed assets, such as factories, machinery, equipment, dwellings, and inventories of raw materials, which provide the basis for future production. It is measured gross of the depreciation of the assets, i.e., it includes investment that merely replaces worn-out or scrapped capital.

Irrigated land

This entry gives the number of square kilometers of land area that is artificially supplied with water.

J

Judicial branch

This entry contains the name(s) of the highest court(s) and a brief description of the selection process for members.

L

Labor force

This entry contains the total labor force figure.

Labor force - by occupation

This entry lists the percentage distribution of the labor force by occupation. The distribution will total less than 100 percent if the data are incomplete and may range from 99-101 percent due to rounding.

Land boundaries

This entry contains the total length of all land boundaries and the individual lengths for each of the contiguous border countries. When available, official lengths published by national statistical agencies are used. Because surveying methods may differ, country border lengths reported by contiguous countries may differ.

Land use

This entry contains the percentage shares of total land area for three different types of land use: arable land - land cultivated for crops like wheat, maize, and rice that are replanted after each harvest; permanent crops - land cultivated for crops like citrus, coffee, and rubber that are not replanted after each harvest; includes land under flowering shrubs, fruit trees, nut trees, and vines, but excludes land under trees grown for wood or timber; other - any land not arable or under permanent crops; includes permanent meadows and pastures, forests and woodlands, built-on areas, roads, barren land, etc.

Languages

This entry provides a rank ordering of languages starting with the largest and sometimes includes the percent of total population speaking that language.

Legal system

This entry provides the description of a country's legal system; it also includes information on acceptance of International Court of Justice (ICJ) jurisdiction. The legal systems of nearly all countries are generally modeled upon elements of five main types: civil law (including French law, the Napoleonic Code, Roman law, Roman-Dutch law, and Spanish law); common law (including United State law); customary law; mixed or pluralistic law; and religious law (including Islamic law). An additional type of legal system - international law, which governs the conduct of independent nations in their relationships with one another - is also addressed below. The following list describes these legal systems, the countries or world regions where these systems are enforced, and a brief statement on the origins and major features of each. Civil Law - The most widespread type of legal system in the world, applied in various forms in approximately 150 countries. Also referred to as European continental law, the civil law system is derived mainly from the Roman Corpus Juris Civilus, (Body of Civil Law), a collection of laws and legal interpretations compiled under the East Roman (Byzantine) Emperor Justinian I between A.D. 528 and 565. The major feature of civil law systems is that the laws are organized into systematic written codes. In civil law the sources recognized as authoritative are principally legislation - especially codifications in constitutions or statutes enacted by governments - and secondarily, custom. The civil law systems in some countries are based on more than one code. Common Law - A type of legal system, often synonymous with "English common law," which is the system of England and Wales in the UK, and is also in force in approximately 80 countries formerly part of or influenced by the former British Empire. English common law reflects Biblical influences as well as remnants of law systems imposed by early conquerors including the Romans, Anglo-Saxons, and Normans. Some legal scholars attribute the formation of the English common law system to King Henry II (r.1154-1189). Until the time of his reign, laws customary among England's various manorial and ecclesiastical (church) jurisdictions were administered locally. Henry II established the king's court and designated that laws were "common" to the entire English realm. The foundation of English common law is "legal precedent" - referred to as stare decisis, meaning "to stand by things decided." In the English common law system, court judges are bound in their decisions in large part by the rules and other doctrines developed - and supplemented over time - by the judges of earlier English courts. Customary Law - A type of legal system that serves as the basis of, or has influenced, the present-day laws in approximately 40 countries - mostly in Africa, but some in the Pacific islands, Europe, and the Near East. Customary law is also referred to as "primitive law," "unwritten law," "indigenous law," and "folk law." There is no single history of customary law such as that found in Roman civil law, English common law, Islamic law, or the Napoleonic Civil Code. The earliest systems of law in human society were customary, and usually developed in small agrarian and hunter-gatherer communities. As the term implies, customary law is based upon the customs of a community. Common attributes of customary legal systems are that they are seldom written down, they embody an organized set of rules regulating social relations, and they are agreed upon by members of the community. Although such law systems include sanctions for law infractions, resolution tends to be reconciliatory rather than punitive. A number of African states practiced customary law many centuries prior to colonial influences. Following colonization, such laws were written down and incorporated to varying extents into the legal systems imposed by their colonial powers. European Union Law - A sub-discipline of international law known as "supranational law" in which the rights of sovereign nations are limited in relation to one another. Also referred to as the Law of the European Union or Community Law, it is the unique and complex legal system that operates in tandem with the laws of the 27 member states of the European Union (EU). Similar to federal states, the EU legal system ensures compliance from the member states because of the Union's decentralized political nature. The European Court of Justice

(ECJ), established in 1952 by the Treaty of Paris, has been largely responsible for the development of EU law. Fundamental principles of European Union law include: subsidiarity - the notion that issues be handled by the smallest, lowest, or least centralized competent authority; proportionality - the EU may only act to the extent needed to achieve its objectives; conferral - the EU is a union of member states, and all its authorities are voluntarily granted by its members; legal certainty - requires that legal rules be clear and precise; and precautionary principle - a moral and political principle stating that if an action or policy might cause severe or irreversible harm to the public or to the environment, in the absence of a scientific consensus that harm would not ensue, the burden of proof falls on those who would advocate taking the action. French Law - A type of civil law that is the legal system of France. The French system also serves as the basis for, or is mixed with, other legal systems in approximately 50 countries, notably in North Africa, the Near East, and the French territories and dependencies. French law is primarily codified or systematic written civil law. Prior to the French Revolution (1789-1799), France had no single national legal system. Laws in the northern areas of present-day France were mostly local customs based on privileges and exemptions granted by kings and feudal lords, while in the southern areas Roman law predominated. The introduction of the Napoleonic Civil Code during the reign of Napoleon I in the first decade of the 19th century brought major reforms to the French legal system, many of which remain part of France's current legal structure, though all have been extensively amended or redrafted to address a modern nation. French law distinguishes between "public law" and "private law." Public law relates to government, the French Constitution, public administration, and criminal law. Private law covers issues between private citizens or corporations. The most recent changes to the French legal system - introduced in the 1980s - were the decentralization laws, which transferred authority from centrally appointed government representatives to locally elected representatives of the people. International Law - The law of the international community, or the body of customary rules and treaty rules accepted as legally binding by states in their relations with each other. International law differs from other legal systems in that it primarily concerns sovereign political entities. There are three separate disciplines of international law: public international law, which governs the relationship between provinces and international entities and includes treaty law, law of the sea, international criminal law, and international humanitarian law; private international law, which addresses legal jurisdiction; and supranational law - a legal framework wherein countries are bound by regional agreements in which the laws of the member countries are held inapplicable when in conflict with supranational laws. At present the European Union is the only entity under a supranational legal system. The term "international law" was coined by Jeremy Bentham in 1780 in his Principles of Morals and Legislation, though laws governing relations between states have been recognized from very early times (many centuries B.C.). Modern international law developed alongside the emergence and growth of the European nation-states beginning in the early 16th century. Other factors that influenced the development of international law included the revival of legal studies, the growth of international trade, and the practice of exchanging emissaries and establishing legations. The sources of International law are set out in Article 38-1 of the Statute of the International Court of Justice within the UN Charter. Islamic Law - The most widespread type of religious law, it is the legal system enforced in over 30 countries, particularly in the Near East, but also in Central and South Asia, Africa, and Indonesia. In many countries Islamic law operates in tandem with a civil law system. Islamic law is embodied in the sharia, an Arabic word meaning "the right path." Sharia covers all aspects of public and private life and organizes them into five categories: obligatory, recommended, permitted, disliked, and forbidden. The primary sources of sharia law are the Qur'an, believed by Muslims to be the word of God revealed to the Prophet Muhammad by the angel Gabriel, and the Sunnah, the teachings of the Prophet and his works. In addition to these two primary sources, traditional Sunni Muslims recognize the consensus of Muhammad's companions and Islamic jurists on certain issues, called ijmas, and various forms of reasoning, including analogy by legal scholars, referred to as qiyas. Shia Muslims reject ijmas and qiyas as sources of sharia law. Mixed Law - Also referred to as pluralistic law, mixed law consists of elements of some or all of the other main types of legal systems - civil, common, customary, and religious. The mixed legal systems of a number of countries came about when colonial powers overlaid their own legal systems upon colonized regions but retained elements of the colonies' existing legal systems. Napoleonic Civil Code - A type of civil law, referred to as the Civil Code or Code Civil des Francais, forms part of the legal system of France, and underpins the legal systems of Bolivia, Egypt, Lebanon, Poland, and the US state of Louisiana. The Civil Code was established under Napoleon I, enacted in 1804, and officially designated the Code Napoleon in 1807. This legal system combined the Teutonic civil law tradition of the northern provinces of France with the Roman law tradition of the southern and eastern regions of the country. The Civil Code bears similarities in its arrangement to the Roman Body of Civil Law (see Civil Law above). As enacted in 1804, the Code addressed personal status, property, and the acquisition of property. Codes added over the following six years included civil procedures, commercial law, criminal law and procedures, and a penal code. Religious Law - A legal system which stems from the sacred texts of religious traditions and in most cases professes to cover all aspects of life as a seamless part of devotional obligations to a transcendent, imminent, or deep philosophical reality. Implied as the basis of religious law is the concept of unalterability, because the word of God cannot be amended or legislated against by judges or governments. However, a detailed legal system generally requires human elaboration. The main types of religious law are sharia in Islam, halakha in Judaism, and canon law in some Christian groups. Sharia is the most widespread religious legal system (see Islamic Law), and is the sole system of law for countries including Iran, the Maldives, and Saudi Arabia. No country is fully governed by halakha, but Jewish people may decide to settle disputes through Jewish courts and be bound by their rulings. Canon law is not a divine law as such because it is not found in revelation. It is viewed instead as human law inspired by the word of God and applying the demands of that revelation to the actual situation of the church. Canon law regulates the internal ordering of the Roman Catholic Church, the Eastern Orthodox Church, and the Anglican Communion. Roman Law - A type of civil law developed in ancient Rome and practiced from the time of the city's founding (traditionally 753 B.C.) until the fall of the Western Empire in the 5th century A.D. Roman law remained the legal system of the Byzantine (Eastern Empire) until the fall of Constantinople in 1453. Preserved fragments of the first legal text, known as the Law of the Twelve Tables, dating from the 5th century B.C., contained specific provisions designed to change the prevailing customary law. Early Roman law was drawn from custom and statutes; later, during the time of the empire, emperors asserted their authority as the ultimate source of law. The basis for Roman laws was the idea that the exact form - not the intention - of words or of actions produced legal consequences. It was only in the late 6th century A.D. that a comprehensive Roman code of laws was published (see Civil Law above). Roman law served as the basis of law systems developed in a number of continental European countries. Roman-Dutch Law - A type of civil law based on Roman law as applied in the Netherlands. Roman-Dutch law serves as the basis for legal systems in seven African countries, as well as Guyana, Indonesia, and Sri Lanka. This law system, which originated in the province of Holland and expanded throughout the Netherlands (to be replaced by the French Civil Code in 1809), was instituted in a number of sub-Saharan African countries during the Dutch colonial period. The Dutch jurist/philosopher Hugo Grotius was the first to attempt to reduce Roman-Dutch civil law into a system in his Jurisprudence of Holland (written 1619-20, commentary published 1621). The Dutch historian/lawyer Simon van Leeuwen coined the term "Roman-Dutch law" in 1652. Spanish Law - A type of civil law, often referred to as the Spanish Civil Code, it is the present legal system of Spain and is the basis of legal systems in 12 countries mostly in Central and South America, but also in southwestern Europe, northern and western Africa, and southeastern Asia. The Spanish Civil Code reflects a complex mixture of customary, Roman, Napoleonic, local, and modern codified law. The laws of the Visigoth invaders of Spain in the 5th to 7th centuries had the earliest major influence on Spanish legal system development. The Christian Reconquest of Spain in the 11th through 15th centuries witnessed the development of customary law, which combined canon (religious) and Roman law. During several centuries of Hapsburg and Bourbon rule, systematic recompilations of the existing national legal system were attempted, but these often conflicted with local and regional customary civil laws. Legal system development for most of the 19th century concentrated on formulating a national civil law system, which was finally enacted in 1889 as the Spanish Civil Code. Several sections of the code have been revised, the most recent of which are the penal code in 1989 and the judiciary code in 2001. The Spanish Civil Code separates public and private law. Public law includes constitutional law, administrative law, criminal law, process law, financial and tax law, and international public law. Private law includes civil law, commercial law, labor law, and international private law. United States Law - A type of common law, which is the basis of the legal system of the United States and that of its island possessions in the Caribbean and the Pacific. This legal system has several layers, more possibly than in most other countries, and is due in part to the division between federal and state law. The United States was founded not as one nation but as a union of 13 colonies, each claiming independence from the British Crown. The US Constitution, implemented in 1789, began shifting power away from the states and toward the federal government, though the states today retain substantial legal authority. US law draws its authority from four sources: constitutional law, statutory law, administrative regulations, and case law. Constitutional law is based on the US Constitution and serves as the supreme federal law. Taken together with those of the state constitutions, these documents outline the general structure of the federal and state governments and provide the rules and limits of power. US statutory law is legislation enacted by the US Congress and is codified in the United States Code. The 50 state legislatures have similar authority to enact state statutes. Administrative law is the authority delegated to federal and state executive agencies. Case law, also referred to as common law, covers areas where constitutional or statutory law is lacking. Case law is a collection of judicial decisions, customs, and general principles that began in England centuries ago, that were adopted in America at the time of the Revolution, and that continue to develop today.

Legislative branch

This entry contains information on the structure (unicameral, bicameral, tricameral), formal name, number of seats, and term of office. Elections includes the nature of the election process or accession to power, date of the last election, and date of the next election. Election results includes the percent of vote and/or number of seats held by each party in the last election.

Life expectancy at birth

This entry contains the average number of years to be lived by a group of people born in the same year, if mortality at each age remains constant in the future. The entry includes total population as well as the male and female components. Life expectancy at birth is also a measure of overall quality of life in a country and summarizes the mortality at all ages. It can also be thought of as indicating the potential return on investment in human capital and is necessary for the calculation of various actuarial measures.

Literacy

This entry includes a definition of literacy and Census Bureau percentages for the total population, males, and females. There are no universal definitions and standards of literacy. Unless otherwise specified, all rates are based on the most common definition - the ability to read and write at a specified age. Detailing the standards that individual countries use to assess the ability to read and write is beyond the scope of the Factbook. Information on literacy, while not a perfect measure of educational results, is probably the most easily available and valid for international comparisons. Low levels of literacy, and education in general, can impede the economic development of a country in the current rapidly changing, technology-driven world.

Location

This entry identifies the country's regional location, neighboring countries, and adjacent bodies of water.

M

Major infectious diseases

This entry lists major infectious diseases likely to be encountered in countries where the risk of such diseases is assessed to be very high as compared to the United States. These infectious diseases represent risks to US government personnel traveling to the specified country for a period of less than three years. The degree of risk is assessed by considering the foreign nature of these infectious diseases, their severity, and the probability of being affected by the diseases present. The diseases listed do not necessarily represent the total disease burden experienced by the local population. The risk to an individual traveler varies considerably by the specific location, visit duration, type of activities, type of accommodations, time of year, and other factors. Consultation with a travel medicine physician is needed to evaluate individual risk and recommend appropriate preventive measures such as vaccines. Diseases are organized into the following six exposure categories shown in italics and listed in typical descending order of risk. Note: The sequence of exposure categories listed in individual country entries may vary according to local conditions. food or waterborne diseases acquired through eating or drinking on the local economy: Hepatitis A - viral disease that interferes with the functioning of the liver; spread through consumption of food or water contaminated with fecal matter, principally in areas of poor sanitation; victims exhibit fever, jaundice, and diarrhea; 15% of victims will experience prolonged symptoms over 6-9 months; vaccine available. Hepatitis E - waterborne viral disease that interferes with the functioning of the liver; most commonly spread through fecal contamination of drinking water; victims exhibit jaundice, fatigue, abdominal pain, and dark colored urine. Typhoid fever - bacterial disease spread through contact with food or water contaminated by fecal matter or sewage; victims exhibit sustained high fevers; left untreated, mortality rates can reach 20%. vectorborne diseases acquired through the bite of an infected arthropod: Malaria - caused by single-cell parasitic protozoa Plasmodium; transmitted to humans via the bite of the female Anopheles mosquito;

parasites multiply in the liver attacking red blood cells resulting in cycles of fever, chills, and sweats accompanied by anemia; death due to damage to vital organs and interruption of blood supply to the brain; endemic in 100, mostly tropical, countries with 90% of cases and the majority of 1.5-2.5 million estimated annual deaths occurring in sub-Saharan Africa. Dengue fever - mosquito-borne (Aedes aegypti) viral disease associated with urban environments; manifests as sudden onset of fever and severe headache; occasionally produces shock and hemorrhage leading to death in 5% of cases. Yellow fever - mosquito-borne viral disease; severity ranges from influenza-like symptoms to severe hepatitis and hemorrhagic fever; occurs only in tropical South America and sub-Saharan Africa, where most cases are reported; fatality rate is less than 20%. Japanese Encephalitis - mosquito-borne (Culex tritaeniorhynchus) viral disease associated with rural areas in Asia; acute encephalitis can progress to paralysis, coma, and death; fatality rates 30%. African Trypanosomiasis - caused by the parasitic protozoa Trypanosoma; transmitted to humans via the bite of bloodsucking Tsetse flies; infection leads to malaise and irregular fevers and, in advanced cases when the parasites invade the central nervous system, coma and death; endemic in 36 countries of sub-Saharan Africa; cattle and wild animals act as reservoir hosts for the parasites. Cutaneous Leishmaniasis - caused by the parasitic protozoa leishmania; transmitted to humans via the bite of sandflies; results in skin lesions that may become chronic; endemic in 88 countries; 90% of cases occur in Iran, Afghanistan, Syria, Saudi Arabia, Brazil, and Peru; wild and domesticated animals as well as humans can act as reservoirs of infection. Plague - bacterial disease transmitted by fleas normally associated with rats; person-to-person airborne transmission also possible; recent plague epidemics occurred in areas of Asia, Africa, and South America associated with rural areas or small towns and villages; manifests as fever, headache, and painfully swollen lymph nodes; disease progresses rapidly and without antibiotic treatment leads to pneumonic form with a death rate in excess of 50%. Crimean-Congo hemorrhagic fever - tick-borne viral disease; infection may also result from exposure to infected animal blood or tissue; geographic distribution includes Africa, Asia, the Middle East, and Eastern Europe; sudden onset of fever, headache, and muscle aches followed by hemorrhaging in the bowels, urine, nose, and gums; mortality rate is approximately 30%. Rift Valley fever - viral disease affecting domesticated animals and humans; transmission is by mosquito and other biting insects; infection may also occur through handling of infected meat or contact with blood; geographic distribution includes eastern and southern Africa where cattle and sheep are raised; symptoms are generally mild with fever and some liver abnormalities, but the disease may progress to hemorrhagic fever, encephalitis, or ocular disease; fatality rates are low at about 1% of cases. Chikungunya - mosquito-borne (Aedes aegypti) viral disease associated with urban environments, similar to Dengue Fever; characterized by sudden onset of fever, rash, and severe joint pain usually lasting 3-7 days, some cases result in persistent arthritis. water contact diseases acquired through swimming or wading in freshwater lakes, streams, and rivers: Leptospirosis - bacterial disease that affects animals and humans; infection occurs through contact with water, food, or soil contaminated by animal urine; symptoms include high fever, severe headache, vomiting, jaundice, and diarrhea; untreated, the disease can result in kidney damage, liver failure, meningitis, or respiratory distress; fatality rates are low but left untreated recovery can take months. Schistosomiasis - caused by parasitic trematode flatworm Schistosoma; fresh water snails act as intermediate host and release larval form of parasite that penetrates the skin of people exposed to contaminated water; worms mature and reproduce in the blood vessels, liver, kidneys, and intestines releasing eggs, which become trapped in tissues triggering an immune response; may manifest as either urinary or intestinal disease resulting in decreased work or learning capacity; mortality, while generally low, may occur in advanced cases usually due to bladder cancer; endemic in 74 developing countries with 80% of infected people living in sub-Saharan Africa; humans act as the reservoir for this parasite. aerosolized dust or soil contact disease acquired through inhalation of aerosols contaminated with rodent urine: Lassa fever - viral disease carried by rats of the genus Mastomys; endemic in portions of West Africa; infection occurs through direct contact with or consumption of food contaminated by rodent urine or fecal matter containing virus particles; fatality rate can reach 50% in epidemic outbreaks. respiratory disease acquired through close contact with an infectious person: Meningococcal meningitis - bacterial disease causing an inflammation of the lining of the brain and spinal cord; one of the most important bacterial pathogens is Neisseria meningitidis because of its potential to cause epidemics; symptoms include stiff neck, high fever, headaches, and vomiting; bacteria are transmitted from person to person by respiratory droplets and facilitated by close and prolonged contact resulting from crowded living conditions, often with a seasonal distribution; death occurs in 5-15% of cases, typically within 24-48 hours of onset of symptoms; highest burden of meningococcal disease occurs in the hyperendemic region of sub-Saharan Africa known as the "Meningitis Belt" which stretches from Senegal east to Ethiopia. animal contact disease acquired through direct contact with local animals: Rabies - viral disease of mammals usually transmitted through the bite of an infected animal, most commonly dogs; virus affects the central nervous system causing brain alteration and death; symptoms initially are non-specific fever and headache progressing to neurological symptoms; death occurs within days of the onset of symptoms.

Manpower available for military service

This entry gives the number of males and females falling in the military age range for a country (defined as being ages 16-49) and assumes that every individual is fit to serve.

Manpower fit for military service

This entry gives the number of males and females falling in the military age range for a country (defined as being ages 16-49) and who are not otherwise disqualified for health reasons; accounts for the health situation in the country and provides a more realistic estimate of the actual number fit to serve.

Manpower reaching militarily significant age annually

This entry gives the number of males and females entering the military manpower pool (i.e., reaching age 16) in any given year and is a measure of the availability of military-age young adults.

Map references

This entry includes the name of the Factbook reference map on which a country may be found. Note that boundary representations on these maps are not necessarily authoritative. The entry on Geographic coordinates may be helpful in finding some smaller countries.

Maritime claims

This entry includes the following claims, the definitions of which are excerpted from the United Nations Convention on the Law of the Sea (UNCLOS), which alone contains the full and definitive descriptions: territorial sea - the sovereignty of a coastal state extends beyond its land territory and internal waters to an adjacent belt of sea, described as the territorial sea in the UNCLOS (Part II); this sovereignty extends to the air space over the territorial sea as well as its underlying seabed and subsoil; every state has the right to establish the breadth of its territorial sea up to a limit not exceeding 12 nautical miles; the normal baseline for measuring the breadth of the territorial sea is the mean low-water line along the coast as marked on large-scale charts officially recognized by the coastal state; the UNCLOS describes specific rules for archipelagic states. contiguous zone - according to the UNCLOS (Article 33), this is a zone contiguous to a coastal state's territorial sea, over which it may exercise the control necessary to: prevent infringement of its customs, fiscal, immigration, or sanitary laws and regulations within its territory or territorial sea; punish infringement of the above laws and regulations committed within its territory or territorial sea; the contiguous zone may not extend beyond 24 nautical miles from the baselines from which the breadth of the territorial sea is measured (e.g. the US has claimed a 12-nautical mile contiguous zone in addition to its 12-nautical mile territorial sea). exclusive economic zone (EEZ) - the UNCLOS (Part V) defines the EEZ as a zone beyond and adjacent to the territorial sea in which a coastal state has: sovereign rights for the purpose of exploring and exploiting, conserving and managing the natural resources, whether living or non-living, of the waters superjacent to the seabed and of the seabed and its subsoil, and with regard to other activities for the economic exploitation and exploration of the zone, such as the production of energy from the water, currents, and winds; jurisdiction with regard to the establishment and use of artificial islands, installations, and structures; marine scientific research; the protection and preservation of the marine environment; the outer limit of the exclusive economic zone shall not exceed 200 nautical miles from the baselines from which the breadth of the territorial sea is measured. continental shelf - the UNCLOS (Article 76) defines the continental shelf of a coastal state as comprising the seabed and subsoil of the submarine areas that extend beyond its territorial sea throughout the natural prolongation of its land territory to the outer edge of the continental margin, or to a distance of 200 nautical miles from the baselines from which the breadth of the territorial sea is measured where the outer edge of the continental margin does not extend up to that distance; the continental margin comprises the submerged prolongation of the landmass of the coastal state, and consists of the seabed and subsoil of the shelf, the slope and the rise; wherever the continental margin extends beyond 200 nautical miles from the baseline, coastal states may extend their claim to a distance not to exceed 350 nautical miles from the baseline or 100 nautical miles from the 2500 meter isobath; it does not include the deep ocean floor with its oceanic ridges or the subsoil thereof. exclusive fishing zone - while this term is not used in the UNCLOS, some states (e.g., the United Kingdom) have chosen not to claim an EEZ, but rather to claim jurisdiction over the living resources off their coast; in such cases, the term exclusive fishing zone is often used; the breadth of this zone is normally the same as the EEZ or 200 nautical miles.

Market value of publicly traded shares

This entry gives the value of shares issued by publicly traded companies at a price determined in the national stock markets on the final day of the period indicated. It is simply the latest price per share multiplied by the total number of outstanding shares, cumulated over all companies listed on the particular exchange.

Median age

This entry is the age that divides a population into two numerically equal groups; that is, half the people are younger than this age and half are older. It is a single index that summarizes the age distribution of a population. Currently, the median age ranges from a low of about 15 in Uganda and Gaza Strip to 40 or more in several European countries and Japan. See the entry for "Age structure" for the importance of a young versus an older age structure and, by implication, a low versus a higher median age.

Merchant marine

Merchant marine may be defined as all ships engaged in the carriage of goods; or all commercial vessels (as opposed to all nonmilitary ships), which excludes tugs, fishing vessels, offshore oil rigs, etc. This entry contains information in four fields - total, ships by type, foreign-owned, and registered in other countries. Total includes the number of ships (1,000 GRT or over), total DWT for those ships, and total GRT for those ships. DWT or dead weight tonnage is the total weight of cargo, plus bunkers, stores, etc., that a ship can carry when immersed to the appropriate load line. GRT or gross register tonnage is a figure obtained by measuring the entire sheltered volume of a ship available for cargo and passengers and converting it to tons on the basis of 100 cubic feet per ton; there is no stable relationship between GRT and DWT. Ships by type includes a listing of barge carriers, bulk cargo ships, cargo ships, chemical tankers, combination bulk carriers, combination ore/oil carriers, container ships, liquefied gas tankers, livestock carriers, multifunctional large-load carriers, petroleum tankers, passenger ships, passenger/cargo ships, railcar carriers, refrigerated cargo ships, roll-on/roll-off cargo ships, short-sea passenger ships, specialized tankers, and vehicle carriers. Foreign-owned are ships that fly the flag of one country but belong to owners in another. Registered in other countries are ships that belong to owners in one country but fly the flag of another.

Military

This category includes the entries dealing with a country's military structure, manpower, and expenditures.

Military - note

This entry includes miscellaneous military information of significance not included elsewhere.

Military branches

This entry lists the service branches subordinate to defense ministries or the equivalent (typically ground, naval, air, and marine forces).

Military expenditures

This entry gives spending on defense programs for the most recent year available as a percent of gross domestic product (GDP); the GDP is calculated on an exchange rate basis, i.e., not in terms of purchasing power parity (PPP).

Military service age and obligation

This entry gives the required ages for voluntary or conscript military service and the length of service obligation.

Money figures

All money figures are expressed in contemporaneous US dollars unless otherwise indicated.

N

National anthem

A generally patriotic musical composition - usually in the form of a song or hymn of praise - that evokes and eulogizes the history, traditions, or struggles of a nation or its people. National anthems can be officially recognized as a national song by a country's constitution or by an enacted law, or simply by tradition. Although most anthems contain lyrics, some do not.

National holiday

This entry gives the primary national day of celebration - usually independence day.

Nationality

This entry provides the identifying terms for citizens - noun and adjective.

Natural gas - consumption

This entry is the total natural gas consumed in cubic meters (cu m). The discrepancy between the amount of natural gas produced and/or imported and the amount consumed and/or exported is due to the omission of stock changes and other complicating factors.

Natural gas - exports

This entry is the total natural gas exported in cubic meters (cu m).

Natural gas - imports

This entry is the total natural gas imported in cubic meters (cu m).

Natural gas - production

This entry is the total natural gas produced in cubic meters (cu m). The discrepancy between the amount of natural gas produced and/or imported and the amount consumed and/or exported is due to the omission of stock changes and other complicating factors.

Natural gas - proved reserves

This entry is the stock of proved reserves of natural gas in cubic meters (cu m). Proved reserves are those quantities of natural gas, which, by analysis of geological and engineering data, can be estimated with a high degree of confidence to be commercially recoverable from a given date forward, from known reservoirs and under current economic conditions.

Natural hazards

This entry lists potential natural disasters. For countries where volcanic activity is common, a volcanism subfield highlights historically active volcanoes.

Natural resources

This entry lists a country's mineral, petroleum, hydropower, and other resources of commercial importance, such as rare earth elements (REEs).

Net migration rate

This entry includes the figure for the difference between the number of persons entering and leaving a country during the year per 1,000 persons (based on midyear population). An excess of persons entering the country is referred to as net immigration (e.g., 3.56 migrants/1,000 population); an excess of persons leaving the country as net emigration (e.g., -9.26 migrants/1,000 population). The net migration rate indicates the contribution of migration to the overall level of population change. The net migration rate does not distinguish between economic migrants, refugees, and other types of migrants nor does it distinguish between lawful migrants and undocumented migrants.

O

Oil - consumption

This entry is the total oil consumed in barrels per day (bbl/day). The discrepancy between the amount of oil produced and/or imported and the amount consumed and/or exported is due to the omission of stock changes, refinery gains, and other complicating factors.

Oil - exports

This entry is the total oil exported in barrels per day (bbl/day), including both crude oil and oil products.

Oil - imports

This entry is the total oil imported in barrels per day (bbl/day), including both crude oil and oil products.

Oil - production

This entry is the total oil produced in barrels per day (bbl/day). The discrepancy between the amount of oil produced and/or imported and the amount consumed and/or exported is due to the omission of stock changes, refinery gains, and other complicating factors.

Oil - proved reserves

This entry is the stock of proved reserves of crude oil in barrels (bbl). Proved reserves are those quantities of petroleum which, by analysis of geological and engineering data, can be estimated with a high degree of confidence to be commercially recoverable from a given date forward, from known reservoirs and under current economic conditions.

P

People

This category includes the entries dealing with the characteristics of the people and their society.

People - note

This entry includes miscellaneous demographic information of significance not included elsewhere.

Personal Names - Capitalization

The Factbook capitalizes the surname or family name of individuals for the convenience of our users who are faced with a world of different cultures and naming conventions. The need for capitalization, bold type, underlining, italics, or some other indicator of the individual's surname is apparent in the following examples: MAO Zedong, Fidel CASTRO Ruz, George W. BUSH, and TUNKU SALAHUDDIN Abdul Aziz Shah ibni Al-Marhum Sultan Hisammuddin Alam Shah. By knowing the surname, a short form without all capital letters can be used with confidence as in President Castro, Chairman Mao, President Bush, or Sultan Tunku Salahuddin. The same system of capitalization is extended to the names of leaders with surnames that are not commonly used such as Queen ELIZABETH II. For Vietnamese names, the given name is capitalized because officials are referred to by their given name rather than by their surname. For example, the president of Vietnam is Tran Duc LUONG. His surname is Tran, but he is referred to by his given name - President LUONG.

Personal Names - Spelling

The romanization of personal names in the Factbook normally follows the same transliteration system used by the US Board on Geographic Names for spelling place names. At times, however, a foreign leader expressly indicates a preference for, or the media or official documents regularly use, a romanized spelling that differs from the transliteration derived from the US Government standard. In such cases, the Factbook uses the alternative spelling.

Personal Names - Titles

The Factbook capitalizes any valid title (or short form of it) immediately preceding a person's name. A title standing alone is not capitalized. Examples: President PUTIN and President BUSH are chiefs of state. In Russia, the president is chief of state and the premier is the head of the government, while in the US, the president is both chief of state and head of government.

Petroleum

See entries under Oil.

Petroleum products

See entries under Oil.

Pipelines

This entry gives the lengths and types of pipelines for transporting products like natural gas, crude oil, or petroleum products.

Piracy

Piracy is defined by the 1982 United Nations Convention on the Law of the Sea as any illegal act of violence, detention, or depredation directed against a ship, aircraft, persons, or property in a place outside the jurisdiction of any State. Such criminal acts committed in the territorial waters of a littoral state are generally considered to be armed robbery against ships. Information on piracy may be found, where applicable, in the Transportation - note.

Political parties and leaders

This entry includes a listing of significant political organizations and their leaders.

Political pressure groups and leaders

This entry includes a listing of a country's political, social, labor, or religious organizations that are involved in politics, or that exert political pressure, but whose leaders do not stand for legislative election. International movements or organizations are generally not listed.

Population

This entry gives an estimate from the US Bureau of the Census based on statistics from population censuses, vital statistics registration systems, or sample surveys pertaining to the recent past and on assumptions about future trends. The total population presents one overall measure of the potential impact of the country on the world and within its region. Note: Starting with the 1993 Factbook, demographic estimates for some countries (mostly African) have explicitly taken into account the effects of the growing impact of the HIV/AIDS epidemic. These countries are currently: The Bahamas, Benin, Botswana, Brazil, Burkina Faso, Burma, Burundi, Cambodia, Cameroon, Central African Republic, Democratic Republic of the Congo, Republic of the Congo, Cote d'Ivoire, Ethiopia, Gabon, Ghana, Guyana, Haiti, Honduras, Kenya, Lesotho, Malawi, Mozambique, Namibia, Nigeria, Rwanda, South Africa, Swaziland, Tanzania, Thailand, Togo, Uganda, Zambia, and Zimbabwe.

Population below poverty line

National estimates of the percentage of the population falling below the poverty line are based on surveys of sub-groups, with the results weighted by the number of people in each group. Definitions of poverty vary considerably among nations. For example, rich nations generally employ more generous standards of poverty than poor nations.

Population growth rate

The average annual percent change in the population, resulting from a surplus (or deficit) of births over deaths and the balance of migrants entering and leaving a country. The rate may be positive or negative. The growth rate is a factor in determining how great a burden would be imposed on a country by the changing needs of its people for infrastructure (e.g., schools, hospitals, housing, roads), resources (e.g., food, water, electricity), and jobs. Rapid population growth can be seen as threatening by neighboring countries.

Ports and terminals

This entry lists major ports and terminals primarily on the basis of the amount of cargo tonnage shipped through the facilities on an annual basis. In some instances, the number of containers handled or ship visits were also considered.

Public debt

This entry records the cumulative total of all government borrowings less repayments that are denominated in a country's home currency. Public debt should not be confused with external debt, which reflects the foreign currency liabilities of both the private and public sector and must be financed out of foreign exchange earnings.

R

Railways

This entry states the total route length of the railway network and of its component parts by gauge: broad, standard, narrow, and dual. Other gauges are listed under note.

Rare earth elements

Rare earth elements or REEs are 17 chemical elements that are critical in many of today's high-tech industries. They include lanthanum, cerium, praseodymium, neodymium, promethium, samarium, europium, gadolinium, terbium, dysprosium, holmium, erbium, thulium, ytterbium, lutetium, scandium, and yttrium. Typical applications for REEs include batteries in hybrid cars, fiber optic cables, flat panel displays, and permanent magnets, as well as some defense and medical products.

Reference maps

This section includes world and regional maps.

Refugees and internally displaced persons

This entry includes those persons residing in a country as refugees or internally displaced persons (IDPs). The definition of a refugee according to a United Nations Convention is "a person who is outside his/her country of nationality or habitual residence; has a well-founded fear of persecution because of his/her race, religion, nationality, membership in a particular social group or political opinion; and is unable or unwilling to avail himself/herself of the protection of that country, or to return there, for fear of persecution." The UN established the Office of the UN High Commissioner for Refugees (UNHCR) in 1950 to handle refugee matters worldwide. The UN Relief and Works Agency for Palestine Refugees in the Near East

(UNRWA) has a different operational definition for a Palestinian refugee: "a person whose normal place of residence was Palestine during the period 1 June 1946 to 15 May 1948 and who lost both home and means of livelihood as a result of the 1948 conflict." However, UNHCR also assists some 400,000 Palestinian refugees not covered under the UNRWA definition. The term "internally displaced person" is not specifically covered in the UN Convention; it is used to describe people who have fled their homes for reasons similar to refugees, but who remain within their own national territory and are subject to the laws of that state.

Religions

This entry is an ordered listing of religions by adherents starting with the largest group and sometimes includes the percent of total population. The core characteristics and beliefs of the world's major religions are described below. Baha'i - Founded by Mirza Husayn-Ali (known as Baha'u'llah) in Iran in 1852, Baha'i faith emphasizes monotheism and believes in one eternal transcendent God. Its guiding focus is to encourage the unity of all peoples on the earth so that justice and peace may be achieved on earth. Baha'i revelation contends the prophets of major world religions reflect some truth or element of the divine, believes all were manifestations of God given to specific communities in specific times, and that Baha'u'llah is an additional prophet meant to call all humankind. Bahais are an open community, located worldwide, with the greatest concentration of believers in South Asia. Buddhism - Religion or philosophy inspired by the 5th century B.C. teachings of Siddhartha Gautama (also known as Gautama Buddha "the enlightened one"). Buddhism focuses on the goal of spiritual enlightenment centered on an understanding of Gautama Buddha's Four Noble Truths on the nature of suffering, and on the Eightfold Path of spiritual and moral practice, to break the cycle of suffering of which we are a part. Buddhism ascribes to a karmic system of rebirth. Several schools and sects of Buddhism exist, differing often on the nature of the Buddha, the extent to which enlightenment can be achieved - for one or for all, and by whom - religious orders or laity.

Basic Groupings Theravada Buddhism: The oldest Buddhist school, Theravada is practiced mostly in Sri Lanka, Cambodia, Laos, Burma, and Thailand, with minority representation elsewhere in Asia and the West. Theravadans follow the Pali Canon of Buddha's teachings, and believe that one may escape the cycle of rebirth, worldly attachment, and suffering for oneself; this process may take one or several lifetimes. Mahayana Buddhism, including subsets Zen and Tibetan Buddhism: Forms of Mahayana Buddhism are common in East Asia and Tibet, and parts of the West. Mahayanas have additional scriptures beyond the Pali Canon and believe the Buddha is eternal and still teaching. Unlike Theravada Buddhism, Mahayana schools maintain the Buddha-nature is present in all beings and all will ultimately achieve enlightenment. Christianity - Descending from Judaism, Christianity's central belief maintains Jesus of Nazareth is the promised messiah of the Hebrew Scriptures, and that his life, death, and resurrection are salvific for the world. Christianity is one of the three monotheistic Abrahamic faiths, along with Islam and Judaism, which traces its spiritual lineage to Abraham of the Hebrew Scriptures. Its sacred texts include the Hebrew Bible and the New Testament (or the Christian Gospels). Basic Groupings Catholicism (or Roman Catholicism): This is the oldest established western Christian church and the world's largest single religious body. It is supranational, and recognizes a hierarchical structure with the Pope, or Bishop of Rome, as its head, located at the Vatican. Catholics believe the Pope is the divinely ordered head of the Church from a direct spiritual legacy of Jesus' apostle Peter. Catholicism is comprised of 23 particular Churches, or Rites - one Western (Roman or Latin-Rite) and 22 Eastern. The Latin Rite is by far the largest, making up about 98% of Catholic membership. Eastern-Rite Churches, such as the Maronite Church and the Ukrainian Catholic Church, are in communion with Rome although they preserve their own worship traditions and their immediate hierarchy consists of clergy within their own rite. The Catholic Church has a comprehensive theological and moral doctrine specified for believers in its catechism, which makes it unique among most forms of Christianity. Mormonism (including the Church of Jesus Christ of Latter-Day Saints): Originating in 1830 in the United States under

Joseph Smith, Mormonism is not characterized as a form of Protestant Christianity because it claims additional revealed Christian scriptures after the Hebrew Bible and New Testament. The Book of Mormon maintains there was an appearance of Jesus in the New World following the Christian account of his resurrection, and that the Americas are uniquely blessed continents. Mormonism believes earlier Christian traditions, such as the Roman Catholic, Orthodox, and Protestant reform faiths, are apostasies and that Joseph Smith's revelation of the Book of Mormon is a restoration of true Christianity. Mormons have a hierarchical religious leadership structure, and actively proselytize their faith; they are located primarily in the Americas and in a number of other Western countries. Orthodox Christianity: The oldest established eastern form of Christianity, the Holy Orthodox Church, has a ceremonial head in the Bishop of Constantinople (Istanbul), also known as a Patriarch, but its various regional forms (e.g., Greek Orthodox, Russian Orthodox, Serbian Orthodox, Ukrainian Orthodox) are autocephalous (independent of Constantinople's authority, and have their own Patriarchs). Orthodox churches are highly nationalist and ethnic. The Orthodox Christian faith shares many theological tenets with the Roman Catholic Church, but diverges on some key premises and does not recognize the governing authority of the Pope. Protestant Christianity: Protestant Christianity originated in the 16th century as an attempt to reform Roman Catholicism's practices, dogma, and theology. It encompasses several forms or denominations which are extremely varied in structure, beliefs, relationship to state, clergy, and governance. Many protestant theologies emphasize the primary role of scripture in their faith, advocating individual interpretation of Christian texts without the mediation of a final religious authority such as the Roman Pope. The oldest Protestant Christianities include Lutheranism, Calvinism (Presbyterians), and Anglican Christianity (Episcopalians), which have established liturgies, governing structure, and formal clergy. Other variants on Protestant Christianity, including Pentecostal movements and independent churches, may lack one or more of these elements, and their leadership and beliefs are individualized and dynamic. Hinduism - Originating in the Vedic civilization of India (second and first millennium B.C.), Hinduism is an extremely diverse set of beliefs and practices with no single founder or religious authority. Hinduism has many scriptures; the Vedas, the Upanishads, and the Bhagavad-Gita are among some of the most important. Hindus may worship one or many deities, usually with prayer rituals within their own home. The most common figures of devotion are the gods Vishnu, Shiva, and a mother goddess, Devi. Most Hindus believe the soul, or atman, is eternal, and goes through a cycle of birth, death, and rebirth (samsara) determined by one's positive or negative karma, or the consequences of one's actions. The goal of religious life is to learn to act so as to finally achieve liberation (moksha) of one's soul, escaping the rebirth cycle. Islam - The third of the monotheistic Abrahamic faiths, Islam originated with the teachings of Muhammad in the 7th century. Muslims believe Muhammad is the final of all religious prophets (beginning with Abraham) and that the Qu'ran, which is the Islamic scripture, was revealed to him by God. Islam derives from the word submission, and obedience to God is a primary theme in this religion. In order to live an Islamic life, believers must follow the five pillars, or tenets, of Islam, which are the testimony of faith (shahada), daily prayer (salah), giving alms (zakah), fasting during Ramadan (sawm), and the pilgrimage to Mecca (hajj). Basic Groupings The two primary branches of Islam are Sunni and Shia, which split from each other over a religio-political leadership dispute about the rightful successor to Muhammad. The Shia believe Muhammad's cousin and son-in-law, Ali, was the only divinely ordained Imam (religious leader), while the Sunni maintain the first three caliphs after Muhammad were also legitimate authorities. In modern Islam, Sunnis and Shia continue to have different views of acceptable schools of Islamic jurisprudence, and who is a proper Islamic religious authority. Islam also has an active mystical branch, Sufism, with various Sunni and Shia subsets. Sunni Islam accounts for over 75% of the world's Muslim population. It recognizes the Abu Bakr as the first caliph after Muhammad. Sunni has four schools of Islamic doctrine and law - Hanafi, Maliki, Shafi'i, and Hanbali - which uniquely interpret the Hadith, or recorded oral traditions of Muhammad. A Sunni Muslim may elect to follow any one of these schools, as all are considered equally valid. Shia Islam represents 10-

20% of Muslims worldwide, and its distinguishing feature is its reverence for Ali as an infallible, divinely inspired leader, and as the first Imam of the Muslim community after Muhammad. A majority of Shia are known as "Twelvers," because they believe that the 11 familial successor imams after Muhammad culminate in a 12th Imam (al-Mahdi) who is hidden in the world and will reappear at its end to redeem the righteous. Variants Ismaili faith: A sect of Shia Islam, its adherents are also known as "Seveners," because they believe that the rightful seventh Imam in Islamic leadership was Isma'il, the elder son of Imam Jafar al-Sadiq. Ismaili tradition awaits the return of the seventh Imam as the Mahdi, or Islamic messianic figure. Ismailis are located in various parts of the world, particularly South Asia and the Levant. Alawi faith: Another Shia sect of Islam, the name reflects followers' devotion to the religious authority of Ali. Alawites are a closed, secretive religious group who assert they are Shia Muslims, although outside scholars speculate their beliefs may have a syncretic mix with other faiths originating in the Middle East. Alawis live mostly in Syria, Lebanon, and Turkey. Druze faith: A highly secretive tradition and a closed community that derives from the Ismaili sect of Islam; its core beliefs are thought to emphasize a combination of Gnostic principles believing that the Fatimid caliph, al-Hakin, is the one who embodies the key aspects of goodness of the universe, which are, the intellect, the word, the soul, the preceder, and the follower. The Druze have a key presence in Syria, Lebanon, and Israel. Jainism - Originating in India, Jain spiritual philosophy believes in an eternal human soul, the eternal universe, and a principle of "the own nature of things." It emphasizes compassion for all living things, seeks liberation of the human soul from reincarnation through enlightenment, and values personal responsibility due to the belief in the immediate consequences of one's behavior. Jain philosophy teaches non-violence and prescribes vegetarianism for monks and laity alike; its adherents are a highly influential religious minority in Indian society. Judaism - One of the first known monotheistic religions, likely dating to between 2000-1500 B.C., Judaism is the native faith of the Jewish people, based upon the belief in a covenant of responsibility between a sole omnipotent creator God and Abraham, the patriarch of Judaism's Hebrew Bible, or

Tanakh. Divine revelation of principles and prohibitions in the Hebrew Scriptures form the basis of Jewish law, or halakhah, which is a key component of the faith. While there are extensive traditions of Jewish halakhic and theological discourse, there is no final dogmatic authority in the tradition. Local communities have their own religious leadership. Modern Judaism has three basic categories of faith: Orthodox, Conservative, and Reform/Liberal. These differ in their views and observance of Jewish law, with the Orthodox representing the most traditional practice, and Reform/Liberal communities the most accommodating of individualized interpretations of Jewish identity and faith. Shintoism - A native animist tradition of Japan, Shinto practice is based upon the premise that every being and object has its own spirit or kami. Shinto practitioners worship several particular kamis, including the kamis of nature, and families often have shrines to their ancestors' kamis. Shintoism has no fixed tradition of prayers or prescribed dogma, but is characterized by individual ritual. Respect for the kamis in nature is a key Shinto value. Prior to the end of World War II, Shinto was the state religion of Japan, and bolstered the cult of the Japanese emperor. Sikhism - Founded by the Guru Nanak (born 1469), Sikhism believes in a non-anthropomorphic, supreme, eternal, creator God; centering one's devotion to God is seen as a means of escaping the cycle of rebirth. Sikhs follow the teachings of Nanak and nine subsequent gurus. Their scripture, the Guru Granth Sahib - also known as the Adi Granth - is considered the living Guru, or final authority of Sikh faith and theology. Sikhism emphasizes equality of humankind and disavows caste, class, or gender discrimination. Taoism - Chinese philosophy or religion based upon Lao Tzu's Tao Te Ching, which centers on belief in the Tao, or the way, as the flow of the universe and the nature of things. Taoism encourages a principle of non-force, or wu-wei, as the means to live harmoniously with the Tao. Taoists believe the esoteric world is made up of a perfect harmonious balance and nature, while in the manifest world - particularly in the body - balance is distorted. The Three Jewels of the Tao - compassion, simplicity, and humility - serve as the basis for Taoist ethics. Zoroastrianism - Originating from the teachings of Zoroaster in about the 9th or 10th century B.C., Zoroastrianism may be the oldest continuing creedal religion. Its key beliefs center on a transcendent creator God, Ahura Mazda, and the concept of free will. The key ethical tenets of Zoroastrianism expressed in its scripture, the Avesta, are based on a dualistic worldview where one may prevent chaos if one chooses to serve God and exercises good thoughts, good words, and good deeds. Zoroastrianism is generally a closed religion and members are almost always born to Zoroastrian parents. Prior to the spread of Islam, Zoroastrianism dominated greater Iran. Today, though a minority, Zoroastrians remain primarily in Iran, India, and Pakistan.

Reserves of foreign exchange and gold

This entry gives the dollar value for the stock of all financial assets that are available to the central monetary authority for use in meeting a country's balance of payments needs as of the end-date of the period specified. This category includes not only foreign currency and gold, but also a country's holdings of Special Drawing Rights in the International Monetary Fund, and its reserve position in the Fund.

Roadways

This entry gives the total length of the road network and includes the length of the paved and unpaved portions.

S

School life expectancy (primary to tertiary education)

School life expectancy (SLE) is the total number of years of schooling (primary to tertiary) that a child can expect to receive, assuming that the probability of his or her being enrolled in school at any particular future age is equal to the current enrollment ratio at that age. Caution must be maintained when utilizing this indicator in international comparisons. For example, a year or grade completed in one country is not necessarily the same in terms of educational content or quality as a year or grade completed in another country. SLE represents the expected number of years of schooling that will be completed, including years spent repeating one or more grades.

Sex ratio

This entry includes the number of males for each female in five age groups - at birth, under 15 years, 15-64 years, 65 years and over, and for the total population. Sex ratio at birth has recently emerged as an indicator of certain kinds of sex discrimination in some countries. For instance, high sex ratios at birth in some Asian countries are now attributed to sex-selective abortion and infanticide due to a strong preference for sons. This will affect future marriage patterns and fertility patterns. Eventually, it could cause unrest among young adult males who are unable to find partners.

Stock of broad money

This entry covers all of "Narrow money," plus the total quantity of time and savings deposits, credit union deposits, institutional money market funds, short-term repurchase agreements between the central bank and commercial deposit banks, and other large liquid assets held by nonbank financial institutions, state and local governments, nonfinancial public enterprises, and the private sector of the economy. National currency units have been converted to US dollars at the closing exchange rate for the date of the information. Because of exchange rate movements, changes in money stocks measured in national currency units may vary significantly from those shown in US dollars, and caution is urged when making comparisons over time in US dollars. In addition to serving as a medium of exchange, broad money includes assets that are slightly less liquid than narrow money and the assets tend to function as a "store of value" - a means of holding wealth.

Stock of direct foreign investment - abroad

This entry gives the cumulative US dollar value of all investments in foreign countries made directly by residents - primarily companies - of the home country, as of the end of the time period indicated. Direct investment excludes investment through purchase of shares.

Stock of direct foreign investment - at home

This entry gives the cumulative US dollar value of all investments in the home country made directly by residents - primarily companies - of other countries as of the end of the time period indicated. Direct investment excludes investment through purchase of shares.

Stock of domestic credit

This entry is the total quantity of credit, denominated in the domestic currency, provided by financial institutions to the central bank, state and local governments, public non-financial corporations, and the private sector. The national currency units have been converted to US dollars at the closing exchange rate on the date of the information.

Stock of narrow money

This entry, also know as "M1," comprises the total quantity of currency in circulation (notes and coins) plus demand deposits denominated in the national currency held by nonbank financial institutions, state and local governments, nonfinancial public enterprises, and the private sector of the economy, measured at a specific point in time. National currency units have been converted to US dollars at the closing exchange rate for the date of the information. Because of exchange rate movements, changes in money stocks measured in national currency units may vary significantly from those shown in US dollars, and caution is urged when making comparisons over time in US dollars. Narrow money consists of more liquid assets than broad money and the assets generally function as a "medium of exchange" for an economy.

Suffrage

This entry gives the age at enfranchisement and whether the right to vote is universal or restricted.

T

Telephone numbers

All telephone numbers in The World Factbook consist of the country code in brackets, the city or area code (where required) in parentheses, and the local number. The one component that is not presented is the international access code, which varies from country to country. For example, an international direct dial telephone call placed from the US to Madrid, Spain, would be as follows: 011 [34] (1) 577-xxxx, where 011 is the international access code for station-to-station calls; 01 is for calls other than station-to-station calls, [34] is the country code for Spain, (1) is the city code for Madrid, 577 is the local exchange, and xxxx is the local telephone number. An international direct dial telephone call placed from another country to the US would be as follows: international access code + [1] (202) 939-xxxx, where [1] is the country code for the US, (202) is the area code for Washington, DC, 939 is the local exchange, and xxxx is the local telephone number.

Telephone system

This entry includes a brief general assessment of the system with details on the domestic and international components. The following terms and abbreviations are used throughout the entry: Arabsat - Arab Satellite Communications Organization (Riyadh, Saudi Arabia). Autodin - Automatic Digital Network (US Department of Defense). CB - citizen's band mobile radio communications. Cellular telephone system - the telephones in this system are radio transceivers, with each instrument having its own private radio frequency and sufficient radiated power to reach the booster station in its area (cell), from which the telephone signal is fed to a telephone exchange. Central American Microwave System - a trunk microwave radio relay system that links the countries of Central America and Mexico with each other. Coaxial cable - a multichannel communication cable consisting of a central conducting wire, surrounded by and insulated from a cylindrical conducting shell; a large number of telephone channels can be made available within the insulated space by the use of a large number of carrier frequencies. Comsat - Communications Satellite Corporation (US). DSN - Defense Switched Network (formerly Automatic Voice Network or Autovon); basic general-purpose, switched voice network of the Defense Communications System (US Department of Defense). Eutelsat - European Telecommunications Satellite Organization (Paris). Fiber-optic cable - a multichannel communications cable using a thread of optical glass fibers as a transmission medium in which the signal (voice, video, etc.) is in the form of a coded pulse of light. GSM - a global system for mobile (cellular) communications devised by the Groupe Special Mobile of the pan-European standardization organization, Conference Europeanne des Posts et Telecommunications (CEPT) in 1982. HF - high frequency; any radio frequency in the 3,000- to 30,000-kHz range. Inmarsat - International Maritime Satellite Organization (London); provider of global mobile satellite communications for commercial, distress, and safety applications at sea, in the air, and on land. Intelsat - International Telecommunications Satellite Organization (Washington, DC). Intersputnik - International Organization of Space Communications (Moscow); first established in the former Soviet Union and the East European countries, it is now marketing its services worldwide with earth stations in North America, Africa, and East Asia. Landline - communication wire or cable of any sort that is installed on poles or buried in the ground. Marecs - Maritime European Communications Satellite used in the Inmarsat system on lease from the European Space Agency. Marisat - satellites of the Comsat Corporation that participate in the Inmarsat system. Medarabtel - the Middle East Telecommunications Project of the International Telecommunications Union (ITU) providing a modern telecommunications network, primarily by microwave radio relay, linking Algeria, Djibouti, Egypt, Jordan, Libya, Morocco, Saudi Arabia, Somalia, Sudan, Syria, Tunisia, and Yemen; it was initially started in Morocco in 1970 by the Arab Telecommunications Union (ATU) and was known at that time as the Middle East Mediterranean Telecommunications Network. Microwave radio relay - transmission of long distance telephone calls and television programs by highly directional radio microwaves that are received and sent on from one booster station to another on an optical path. NMT - Nordic Mobile Telephone; an analog cellular telephone system that was developed jointly by the national telecommunications authorities of the Nordic countries (Denmark, Finland, Iceland, Norway, and Sweden). Orbita - a Russian television service; also the trade name of a packet-switched digital telephone network. Radiotelephone communications - the two-way transmission and reception of sounds by broadcast radio on authorized frequencies using telephone handsets. PanAmSat - PanAmSat Corporation (Greenwich, CT). SAFE - South African Far East Cable Satellite communication system - a communication system consisting of two or more earth stations and at least one satellite that provide long distance transmission of voice, data, and television; the system usually serves as a trunk connection between telephone exchanges; if the earth stations are in the same country, it is a domestic system. Satellite earth station - a communications facility with a microwave radio transmitting and receiving antenna and required receiving and transmitting equipment for communicating with satellites. Satellite link - a radio connection between a satellite and an earth station permitting communication between them, either one-way (down link from satellite to earth station - television receive-only transmission) or two-way (telephone channels). SHF - super high frequency; any radio frequency in the 3,000- to 30,000-MHz range. Shortwave - radio frequencies (from 1.605 to 30 MHz) that fall above the commercial broadcast band and are used for communication over long distances. Solidaridad - geosynchronous satellites in Mexico's system of international telecommunications in the Western Hemisphere. Statsionar - Russia's geostationary system for satellite telecommunications. Submarine cable - a cable designed for service under water. TAT - Trans-Atlantic Telephone; any of a number of high-capacity submarine coaxial telephone cables linking Europe with North America. Telefax - facsimile service between subscriber stations via the public switched telephone network or the international Datel network. Telegraph - a telecommunications system designed for unmodulated electric impulse transmission. Telex - a communication service involving teletypewriters connected by wire through automatic exchanges. Tropospheric scatter - a form of microwave radio transmission in which the troposphere is used to scatter and reflect a fraction of the incident radio waves back to earth; powerful, highly directional antennas are used to transmit and receive the microwave signals; reliable over-the-horizon communications are realized for distances up to 600 miles in a single hop; additional hops can extend the range of this system for very long distances. Trunk network - a network of switching centers, connected by multichannel trunk lines. UHF - ultra high frequency; any radio frequency in the 300- to 3,000-MHz range. VHF - very high frequency; any radio frequency in the 30- to 300-MHz range.

Telephones - main lines in use

This entry gives the total number of main telephone lines in use.

Telephones - mobile cellular

This entry gives the total number of mobile cellular telephone subscribers.

Terminology

Due to the highly structured nature of the Factbook database, some collective generic terms have to be used. For example, the word Country in the Country name entry refers to a wide variety of dependencies, areas of special sovereignty, uninhabited islands, and other entities in addition to the traditional countries or independent states. Military is also used as an umbrella term for various civil defense, security, and defense activities in many entries. The Independence entry includes the usual colonial independence dates and former ruling states as well as other significant nationhood dates such as the traditional founding date or the date of unification, federation, confederation, establishment, or state succession that are not strictly independence dates. Dependent areas have the nature of their dependency status noted in this same entry.

Terrain

This entry contains a brief description of the topography.

Time difference

This entry is expressed in The World Factbook in two ways. First, it is stated as the difference in hours between the capital of an entity and Coordinated Universal Time (UTC) during Standard Time. Additionally, the difference in time between the capital of an entity and that observed in Washington, D.C. is also provided. Note that the time difference assumes both locations are simultaneously observing Standard Time or Daylight Saving Time.

Time zones

Ten countries (Australia, Brazil, Canada, Indonesia, Kazakhstan, Mexico, New Zealand, Russia, Spain, and the United States) and the island of Greenland observe more than one official time depending on the number of designated time zones within their boundaries. An illustration of time zones throughout the world and within countries can be seen in the Standard Time Zones of the World map included in the Reference Maps section of The World Factbook.

Total fertility rate

This entry gives a figure for the average number of children that would be born per woman if all women lived to the end of their childbearing years and bore children according to a given fertility rate at each age. The total fertility rate (TFR) is a more direct measure of the level of fertility than the crude birth rate, since it refers to births per woman. This indicator shows the potential for population change in the country. A rate of two children per woman is considered the replacement rate for a population, resulting in relative stability in terms of total numbers. Rates above two children indicate populations growing in size and whose median age is declining. Higher rates may also indicate difficulties for families, in some situations, to feed and educate their children and for women to enter the labor force. Rates below two children indicate populations decreasing in size and growing older. Global fertility rates are in general decline and this trend is most pronounced in industrialized countries, especially Western Europe, where populations are projected to decline dramatically over the next 50 years.

Total renewable water resources

This entry provides the long-term average water availability for a country in cubic kilometers of precipitation, recharged ground water, and surface inflows from surrounding countries. The values have been adjusted to account for overlap resulting from surface flow recharge of groundwater sources. Total renewable water resources provides the water total available to a country but does not include water resource totals that have been reserved for upstream or downstream countries through international agreements. Note that these values are averages and do not accurately reflect the total available in any given year. Annual available resources can vary greatly due to short-term and long-term climatic and weather variations.

Trafficking in persons

Trafficking in persons is modern-day slavery, involving victims who are forced, defrauded, or coerced into labor or sexual exploitation. The International Labor Organization (ILO), the UN agency charged with addressing labor standards, employment, and social protection issues, estimates that 12.3 million people worldwide are enslaved in forced labor, bonded labor, forced child labor, sexual servitude, and involuntary servitude at any given time. Human trafficking is a multi-dimensional threat, depriving people of their human rights and freedoms, risking global health, promoting social breakdown, inhibiting development by depriving countries of their human capital, and helping fuel the growth of organized crime. In 2000, the US Congress passed the Trafficking Victims Protection Act (TVPA), reauthorized in

2003 and 2005, which provides tools for the US to combat trafficking in persons, both domestically and abroad. One of the law's key components is the creation of the US Department of State's annual Trafficking in Persons Report, which assesses the government response (i.e., the current situation) in some 150 countries with a significant number of victims trafficked across their borders who are recruited, harbored, transported, provided, or obtained for forced labor or sexual exploitation. Countries in the annual report are rated in three tiers, based on government efforts to combat trafficking. The countries identified in this entry are those listed in the 2010 Trafficking in Persons Report as Tier 2 Watch List or Tier 3 based on the following tier rating definitions: Tier 2 Watch List countries do not fully comply with the minimum standards for the elimination of trafficking but are making significant efforts to do so, and meet one of the following criteria: 1. they display high or significantly increasing number of victims, 2. they have failed to provide evidence of increasing efforts to combat trafficking in persons, or, 3. they have committed to take action over the next year. Tier 3 countries neither satisfy the minimum standards for the elimination of trafficking nor demonstrate a significant effort to do so. Countries in this tier are subject to potential non-humanitarian and non-trade sanctions.

Transnational issues

This category includes four entries - Disputes - international, Refugees and internally displaced persons, Trafficking in persons, and Illicit drugs - that deal with current issues going beyond national boundaries.

Transportation

This category includes the entries dealing with the means for movement of people and goods.

Transportation - note

This entry includes miscellaneous transportation information of significance not included elsewhere.

U

Unemployment rate

This entry contains the percent of the labor force that is without jobs. Substantial underemployment might be noted.

Urbanization

This entry provides two measures of the degree of urbanization of a population. The first, urban population, describes the percentage of the total population living in urban areas, as defined by the country. The second, rate of urbanization, describes the projected average rate of change of the size of the urban population over the given period of time. Additionally, the World entry includes a list of the ten largest urban agglomerations. An urban agglomeration is defined as comprising the city or town proper and also the suburban fringe or thickly settled territory lying outside of, but adjacent to, the boundaries of the city.

UTC (Coordinated Universal Time)

See entry for Coordinated Universal Time.

W

Waterways

This entry gives the total length of navigable rivers, canals, and other inland bodies of water.

Weights and Measures

This information is presented in This information is presented in <a href = "../appendix/appendix-g.html"Appendix G: Weights and Measures and includes mathematical notations (mathematical powers and names), metric interrelationships (prefix; symbol; length, weight, or capacity; area; volume), and standard conversion factors.

Y

Years

All year references are for the calendar year (CY) unless indicated as fiscal year (FY). The calendar year is an accounting period of 12 months from 1 January to 31 December. The fiscal year is an accounting period of 12 months other than 1 January to 31 December.

End of the book.